Living Beyond Boundaries by Overcoming Obstacles

Malissa C. Stringer

MANIFOLD GRACE
Publishing House LLC

Living Beyond Boundaries by Overcoming Obstacles
Copyright © 2016 Malissa C. Stringer

Cover Design: CreativeLogoArt
Bio Photographer: Carla Bucala

Scriptures taken from KJV Version Bible

ISBN: 978-1-937400-81-1

Printed in the United States of America

Published by Manifold Grace Publishing House, LLC
Southfield, Michigan 48033
www.manifoldgracepublishinghouse.com

Pastor John

Thanks for your support

May your blessings
overflow!!

M. Irving

Dedication

Mommy, this book is dedicated to you. I am so sorry that you did not get to see the finished product. I have worked very hard on this project to make you proud and I know you are smiling down on me every step of the way! I know you are reading the pages as I write them. I know you are very proud of me and my effort to change the lives of each and every person who decides to pick up this book. For every signing and every motivational speech I give, it will all be done in your honor. Thank you for being my very best friend and my biggest cheerleader in everything I ever thought I wanted to do. My life would have never been the same without you. Thank you for every sacrifice you have ever made for me! This one is for you and my children, Lexxis and Kristian. When it was time for you to rest they pushed me, even when I felt like throwing in the towel. Finally, to all of the students whose lives I've managed to touch and change in one way or another, this is also for you!

Thank you all for returning the motivation and inspiration.

Table of Contents

Introduction

Even though seasons change, we must remain consistent. As you read through the chapters of this book it is important to note that, although some chapters may seem irrelevant to you and your situation, please do not skip over them. You see, collectively, the principles discussed throughout this book can effectively be applied as you travel through the seasons of your life. Just as every problem in your life has purpose, the chapters of this book also have a purpose. So, keep reading and be careful not to dismiss what you read. This is food for thought, we are all starving in different areas of our lives and I guarantee you will be fed and satisfied.

When speaking of seasons changing please know I am not speaking of seasons in relation to weather. I am talking about the seasons of life. Consider the seasons when things are well in your life versus those times when everything is out of sorts. Or when you have all the money that you need, versus those times you don't have a dollar in your wallet, purse or bank account. Try, the season of health versus times when illness strikes suddenly. It may be in the season that you have a fantastic job with great coworkers, versus the loss of a job when you're applying to places and everyone says no. Perhaps you are enjoying those you love and the next day they are gone. Additionally, there is that season of life when you thought you'd found the love of your life, only to discover it was a false alarm.

Now that we have a clear understanding about the types of seasons we'll discuss throughout this book, let's move forward to the non-medical prescription of getting through the seasons successfully.

When I began this passage, I spoke of maintaining consistency as the seasons change, which just might catch some of you by surprise. You may wonder how it is possible to remain consistent through the seasons of life. I assure you, it is possible to keep calm through life's storms. As said by G.I. Joe, "Knowing is half the battle." If we know the changes are coming, then we would not be caught off guard when they get here. We all know that life happens and when it does we can't be moved by what we see because we know it is only temporary. We know our source gives us the strength to endure whatever appears to torment us in our lives. No matter what you go through, although you may not understand it, go through with faith and try your best not to be bitter. That will only prolong things. Keep an open mind and know that all things happen according to God's plan. When bad things happen, people have a tendency to give the devil credit, but if you read the word of God you understand that no weapon formed against you shall prosper. Remember, our source is ultimately in control of all things.

1.

The History

I, like many of you, have gone through many things. Life has been a struggle for me. Growing up adopted into a single-parent home, I always felt like the outcast. Unlike many kids who were adopted, I knew my biological mother and siblings. She was abusive. I suffered sexual abuse from the age of three and I didn't know if it was real or not. I never even knew what it felt like to be a virgin. The sexual abuse was at the hand of my biological mother's oldest nephew who was like a brother to her. When she found out about the abuse, she did not believe me. I didn't tell my mother at the time the abuse occurred. I was so young I didn't know if it was a figment of my imagination, or if something truly occurred.

It wasn't until I was 11 years old and he touched me again, that I realized it was not a figment of my imagination. When it happened I snatched away from him, but I still did not tell anyone right away. Finally, I told my sister. My sister was away in Germany with her husband and family, but she took it upon herself to tell my biological mother. She chose to share it with her in a Mother's Day card. That did not go over well for me and made my life difficult for years to come. The abuse followed me throughout my life. I was very promiscuous while growing up, having sex; willingly, the day before my 13th birthday with an 18-year-old man. Fornication led to five pregnancies, which resulted in three abortions and two live births. While thankful for bringing two children into the world, I am often haunted by thoughts of what my other children could've turned out to be. I am sorry to have cut their destinies short.

I began working at the tender age of 14. Life hadn't been easy for me up until this point, but I got out there and did what I had to do. This cycle began with me getting paid under the table at the local pizzeria. I never imagined this would be the beginning of a very long road.

My childhood goal, for as long as I can remember, was to be a lawyer. It was around this time that I came to meet who would end up being my mentor and life coach. My mentor/life coach never wanted the title nor did we realize how far we would go in life together or what a pivotal role she was going to play in my life. That mentor was a guide in so many areas of my life, not only high school, where we met, but her mentoring went on to help me make valuable decisions in my life. She showed me the way to begin college and living life beyond.

When I was in my senior year of high school I got pregnant and it was my mentor who advised me. "I don't know if this is a good idea. You're very young, you have a lot ahead of you and this is just not the right time to bring a child in the world that you can't support." Not only was it not the right time, but the person I was pregnant by was abusive and later ended up in jail for double murder. Strangely enough, three days after I began writing this book, I received a call from the father of the child that I chose to abort over 20 years ago. It's astonishing that he even had the ability to call me. He is still locked away in prison. I found out through speaking with him, that he received two life sentences and had been in prison for the last 20 years, which is primarily the reason I had not heard from him. He found me via Facebook.

My mentor offered to pay for the abortion because I didn't have the money. The date was set and she came to pick up me to have the surgery performed. I struggled with the decision to terminate the pregnancy, however I did undergo the procedure. Although she offered to pay for the abortion, she didn't have to because the procedure was covered under my biological mothers' insurance policy.

After the procedure, I went on to graduate from high school. I wanted to be an attorney but didn't know how I would pay for school, so I thought I'd work first and consider college at a later time. Sheila, my mentor, said "No you're going to college. I will show you a way to get financial aid and whatever financial aid doesn't pay - I will." I was astounded by her generosity. Although neither of us realized it at the time, only God could do a thing like this.

So, in 2001, I went off to community college to work on a degree in criminal justice. I had to work full-time because, at this point, I had my first child and could only go to school part-time. This degree took me five years to complete but with the support of my mentor, cheering me on along the way, I graduated in 2006 with my Associates Degree. At the dinner following graduation, my mentor asked, "Ok, how long is it going to be before you go back to school for your bachelors because you can't stop here." I thought "Wow, can I enjoy and digest this milestone first?"

Later on that year I began working on my Bachelor's degree in Business Management. That degree took a little less than two years to complete and was completed in 2009. It was an online class and graduation was to be held in Chicago. After completing such a huge accomplishment I found myself wondering how to get to graduation. I sure didn't have the additional funds to get to Chicago and pay for a hotel room.

I was so pleased to announce to my mentor that graduation was scheduled for July, but was reluctant to mention an invitation, because I knew there was no way l could afford the trip. However, Sheila saw things differently. She had a daughter who lived in Chicago with her husband and children, and she thought it would be a good idea to, not only go, but to stay with them as well. I was still reluctant because I didn't know what the house was going to be like and I was kind of skeptical about staying at someone else's home; especially someone I did not know. But, I was thankful for the opportunity so I took Sheila up on her offer. Sheila not only took me and my two children, but my Godmother as well.

We arrived at the house and were pleasantly surprised to find a big, beautiful home set on a golf course. It had a 25,000 gallon pool with a beautiful deck, a very nice theater system, personal sauna, and a beautiful winding staircase. It was much more than we could've ever imagined and all at no cost to us. The guest room we stayed in had a 60 inch TV; in 2009 this was not common for most families. Only God could do a thing like this!

2.

Shared Knowledge

"A mentor is someone who allows you to see
the hope inside yourself."
- Oprah Winfrey

Everyone needs someone who will pour wisdom, knowledge and insight into them. Those of us who have had many life experiences, owe it to the generations coming behind us to empty the vault of our experiences into them. Our vaults are filled with wisdom and methods of defeating obstacles and challenges. We are all unique because of the things we have been through. We have so much to offer one another. It is not only the good experiences we have to share, but negative ones also. For example, there was a time in my life that money came very easily and during that time, because I had not had a great deal of capital in my life, I begin to spend recklessly.

I bought things just because I wanted to, not because there was a need. So, I am able to share with you and others that money goes out much easier than it comes in for most people. To that end, if someone comes into a large sum of cash, I encourage you to invest your money wisely and educate yourself on financial discipline, which includes learning to budget your finances and track your spending. So many people, myself included, buy things and then can't figure out what we have spent our money on. By tracking our purchases we can move closer to financial freedom. There are simple tips and tricks that mentors could provide for us. No matter how old you are, we could all use a mentor to increase our wisdom. After all, knowledge is power. We not only have the opportunity to pour into others, but we also need to look for opportunities to soak up knowledge.

If we don't take advantage of life's opportunities we die full and we take wisdom, knowledge, insight and perspective to the grave. That would be awful because the next generation greatly needs what we have to offer. As a matter of fact, we sometimes go through experiences just so we can help someone else who may experience a similar situation. That's why I like to reinforce the point of focusing on the lesson that is to be learned when you are facing an obstacle or challenge. Be willing to talk about your experiences, both good and bad because someone really needs to hear your story. Nothing you have been through, has been a waste of time. Mentors have the wisdom to help you reach your goals and can usually guide your path. They have set goals and accomplished their dreams and aspirations.

It is not absolutely necessary to find a mentor who is successful in an area that you are focusing on. More or less, it is important to find someone who drives you to be great and encourages you to never give up on your dreams. Some people may mistake mentors for life coaches and although they are similar, a life coach is usually someone who is paid. A mentor is someone who values your success and naturally wants to see you win. For a mentor, your success is usually the greatest pay-off ever.

Mentors make an investment into their mentees, because they are an inspiration and are usually great people themselves. They naturally connect with other great people who can be used for networking, which just might propel you into your destiny. This is why you should always be kind to people; you never know when or how opportunities will present themselves. Always be ready, opportunities can show up when you least expect them. Another thing that makes a mentor different, from a network connection, is their commit-ment to you and their desire to see you do well in life.

Good mentors will not only, encourage you to be great, but they will share their own stories of success and triumph. It is always nice to hear my mentor tell me what made her continue to do great things in life. When seeking out a mentor, if you don't already have one, make sure you seek out someone who you admire, as well as someone who inspires you because of their accomplishments. I am sure that if I did not have a mentor, I would not be half the person I am today.

You will know your mentor is 100% genuine if they celebrate your victories, but also if they provide constructive criticism when needed. Your mentor should encourage you to reach your goals - no matter what. Once you reach your goals it is important that your mentor challenges you to set other goals. There should always be a goal for you to aim for, one that will help you become the success that has always been inside of you. One of the greatest things mentors do is help you assess your strengths and weaknesses. They should also challenge you in areas that need development and always provide a fresh perspective. It is nice when you have the ability to look at things from someone else's point of view.

Your mentor, or even you as a mentor, can change the trajectory of someone's life. My mentor, Sheila Greene, certainly did that for me. If she had not been placed in my life I'm not sure where I would have ended up. I can only imagine it would've been a long, ugly road. I am so glad that she looked at me from a perspective that I could not see. It's because of her contribution to my life, that you are able to turn the pages of this book. If you don't have a mentor, get one. If you are not a mentor become one!

3.

Faith Facts

*"Faith is taking the first step even when
you don't see the whole staircase."
– Rev. Martin Luther King, Jr*

"What is this thing called faith?" you ask. Well, let me explain. Faith is believing in something that you don't see. Faith is, not only believing in a higher power such as God or the Universe, but faith can be something as little as believing that the seasons will change. In my experiences, since the diagnosis of cancer, I had to believe in and have faith in the fact that God would heal me. I had to literally speak healing over my life; continuously speaking God's promises. I had to continuously speak positive affirmations over my life for every situation and every aspect of my life. We have to trust Him because He is the finisher of our faith!

It is so important to look at life from the stand-point of having faith against all odds. When you look at it like that, you realize that no weapon formed against you shall prosper. (Isaiah 54:17) Some days we are given devastating news, but we need to find the blessing in it, instead of thriving off of the negative.

When things don't go the way we planned, we should still rejoice and be glad. We should actually celebrate, because most of the time it is truly a blessing that we don't understand until much later. When you stand on God's promises it makes things so much easier. You know that He has your back no matter what the circumstances look like. If only most people stood on their faith and waited patiently until they reached the other side of their issue, they would see His promises fulfilled. It's kind of like waiting for a vacation that has been planned for a very long time; we just need to learn how to rest in His goodness and know that His grace is sufficient.

There are some who don't believe in faith, and oh boy, are they missing out. Having faith greatly depends on the person's relationship with Jesus and the belief that He is indeed God's Son, but also believing that He is everything you need Him to be. We must believe that He is our lawyer in the courtroom, a doctor in the hospital, our mechanic, our healer, our teacher, our pilot and simply – our everything. Sometimes your faith is placed under pressure, but honor God by staying the course.

I have also learned along the way that there is so much power in the tongue. I have to be careful what I speak over my life. For example, my prayer used to consist of me asking that God would make me a living testimony. At the time I prayed that prayer, I did not know what I was truly asking - then I was diagnosed with cancer. It didn't take me long to figure out that this was all a part of God's plan for my life. I had to go through this major test for Him to get the glory. I shared my journey with family, friends and strangers through Facebook. I asked for prayers before my diagnosis, when I got the diagnosis I announced it and asked for continued prayers. I asked that people not feel sorry for me, as it was something I knew I had to go through; but I always believed I would come out of it.

When we are faithful, God is pleased with us. As we go through the challenges of life, there is truly a reward at the end of the struggle. It is difficult to keep our faith when we are going through trials, but that is the time we must stand the strongest. It is up to us to run the race and be faithful, then pass the baton on to our children because they will face challenges as well. We must demonstrate how we respond to challenges and troubles in life. We must show our children through our actions, that no matter what, we are striving to hear God say, "Well done, good and faithful servant." (Matthew 25:23) That is important, our entire life is an act of service. Each day we should make it a point to serve others. We should always help others when we are in a position to do so.

The time will come when we need help. It will not always be the person that we helped who returns the favor, and that is totally fine. One act of service that I find myself practicing is, gathering a full bag of pop bottles. I put them in my car and let them stay in my trunk until I see someone digging bottles out of trash cans. Then, I give them over to him or her. That is an act of kindness that I frequently commit. I am not bragging, I am simply demonstrating what I do as an act of service to others; very simple things can help.

Obstacles that feel like they are choking the life out of you can cause you to behave irrationally. When you feel like your life is out of control, maintain your focus on God. He can and will fight your battles for you. I do mean any situation that you are facing, He's got you, if you just trust Him. When you focus on your obstacles, they are magnified and appear much bigger than they are. We have to learn to relax and realize that storms don't last always.

My sister and son are afraid of storms, but I love them. I actually find peace in storms, so much so that sometimes I sit on my deck until they blow over. They remind me of issues in life, here one minute and gone the next. I'm sure you have witnessed a storm that was pretty rough in nature and immediately following the storm, the sun shines dries up the rain. It looks as if it had never rained. That is a perfect example of life; we go through trials and when they resolve, oftentimes we just don't look like what we have been through. I am certainly a witness to that, because people often tell me that I don't look like I have been through all of the treatment I've had. I simply respond, "It's all because of God's grace!"

The Diagnosis

"Every adversity, every failure, every heartache carries with the seed of an equal or greater benefit."
- Napoleon Hill

In February, 2013 I went to see the doctor that delivered my son 8 years earlier. I visited Dr. P because I was considering allowing him to perform the hysterectomy they suggested to rid me of fibroids in my uterus. Upon seeing Dr. P he asked me if I'd had a recent physical and I told him I had not because I was in the process of switching doctors. Mine had left her practice for reasons unknown.

Since I had not had a recent physical, he decided to do a complete physical which also consisted of a breast exam. Upon doing the exam Dr. P asked if I had ever been told by any physician that I had lumpy breasts? He asked this question because of a condition known as fibrocystic breast. I explained to him that I had not ever been told that, but I did let him know that my doctor, prior to her leaving the practice, explained to me that she wanted me to begin having mammograms at age 35. My family history showed that my mother's sister had breast cancer in her 30's. Dr. P agreed and sent me over for a mammogram, just to check - to be sure. I had the mammogram on February 7, 2013 and they told me that I needed to have an ultrasound. They saw something on the mammogram that confirmed, through the ultrasound, that it was only minor cysts.

Cysts are not uncommon for women, they explained. But there was one cyst that had some type of debris in it that they were concerned about and explained they would aspirate, just to be on the safe side. I was checked two additional times before the actual diagnosis was confirmed. There was a period of time (22 months) where cancer was growing in my body, but I was told I had nothing to be concerned about because what they saw were cysts. The provider gave no indication it was or could have been cancer. I later found out it had indeed been cancer all along.

Miss Likitia was pivotal in helping me find out about my situation. We worked together at a local hospital and one day we had a conversation with a patient who believed in the same faith. During that conversation we talked to the patient about lying on our faces, truly seeking God for the desires of our heart. Miss Likitia said she had to lie out prostrate before the Lord when she was seeking her husband.

I wanted a husband and was seeking God for some

other things in my life, so I decided I would do the same thing and lay down before the Lord. I laid down on the floor in my room, on my left breast and felt like i was lying on a water balloon. I knew then that something just wasn't right, but I trusted my colleagues to point me in the right direction. It is very important to follow your gut, your intuition, no matter what anybody says. Always trust your inner self; never second-guess yourself when you know you're making the right decision. If it were not for Miss Likitia sharing such a personal experience with me, I'm not sure I would be here today to share my story. I am very thankful that God chose her as the person who contributed to saving my life.

After the diagnosis I was excited about starting a new job at an area hospital. I passed the background check and all the requirements related to getting a job. i even went to orientation, only to be told the next day they would not be able to accommodate some upcoming appointments I'd scheduled related to the diagnosis. For a minute, I felt defeated, but I quickly came to the conclusion that God had something better for me. And He was pushing me in that direction, versus allowing me to settle for less than I deserve. I knew God had been dealing with me lately, because I kept telling people that "I have a Master's Degree and instead of applying for administrative assistant jobs, I should be interviewing an administrative assistant to work for me.

God has always given me a mind to do bigger

things and to aim high but I continuously shot below the mark, never consistently focusing on the plans God had for me. I always wanted to be in control instead of allowing God to guide me, but now I had no choice but to surrender it all. That's what He was waiting for me to do. As I am sitting here writing this book, I hear Him saying, "I've got the controls if you just trust me." Trust is such a simple word, yet it has so much power behind it. Trust isn't an easy thing to do when you have been hurt and betrayed by so many. I know that God isn't like people and we (I) have to stop treating Him like He is on their level. His thoughts are not our thoughts. He is not only the Alpha and the Omega, but He knows the beginning and the end of everything!

God can bring encouragement and bring a little light to a very dark situation. When God blesses, you are blessed. God didn't say the trials wouldn't come, only that with Him you can overcome them. He can help you put the enemy on the run. God's going to use the little bit of faith that I have and increase it. Do not doubt yourself. God can do all things, forget the negative report. God is a miracle worker. If you're scared, trust God; He is our source in all situations and circumstances. If God is for you, then who shall be against you? Put your war clothes on it's time for battle. Even though it's time to battle let Him fight your battles and praise Him in advance! Be still and praise God for the victory because He's already won. Thank you Jesus!

Nothing is impossible to him that believes. It is important to have multiple streams of income, because you never know when one will dry up. Most of us are living below our full potential. The greatest tragedy in life is not in death, but a life that fails to fulfill its purpose. We must *"Live fully so you can die effectively"* - Dr. Myles Monroe. Don't just talk about your potential dreams, visions and ideas; make them come to life! People often make many excuses why they can't complete a task or goal. Instead of focusing on the obstacles they should focus on the reason they can get things done.

"You are capable of much more than you were thinking, imagining, doing or being." - Dr. Myles Monroe

Open Doors

"When nothing is sure, everything is possible."
- Margaret Drabble

Have you ever been going through something and God just showed up out of nowhere? It has happened to me several times and I would like to share one of those experiences with you. There was a time when I was concerned about my medical bills during cancer treatments. I had gone to a normal appointment with my oncologist and explained to her how distressed I was over the number of mounting bills I had been receiving. I explained to her that it was simply unbearable. After I finished speaking with her she said, "Stay put, I have someone I need for you to talk to."

At that time I didn't know she was calling the Volunteer Director to come up and have a conversation with me. After waiting for just a little while, a lady named Laura came up to speak with me regarding the concerns I shared with my doctor. I began to tell my story and before l could finish, she tapped me on my knee and said "I can make all that go away, simply bring your bills to me and the other things that you're concerned about and we will take care of them for you." It was like a 10,000 pound weight had been lifted from my shoulders. I knew only God could do a thing like this!

The next day I brought in my bills explaining that I needed assistance with my health insurance at $1,100 a month and also some previous medical bills. Just as she promised, they paid all of my outstanding bills; any incoming bills I would have related to breast cancer; AND paid my health insurance premium for six months. It was absolutely amazing. I did not have to fill out an application for assistance, I did not have to show proof of income and I did not have to release bank statements. The reason that is so significant is, before my meeting with Laura, I sat in my bedroom after a chemotherapy session and found myself calling around for help. Each call resulted in me being told, "Please download this application" or "We will send you an application in the mail, once you complete it and get it back to us we will see if you qualify." Well, I did that time after time and guess what? I never did qualify for one reason or another. To hear her say, "I can make it all go away" when I was at my breaking point - I knew it was nothing more than a move of God. He showed up when I needed Him most and He can, and will, do the same for you.

As a matter of fact I'm sure you have stories of your own where something like this has happened for you. Maybe you did not recognize that it was Him all the time.

Too often we take our miracles for granted, not giving credit to the source from which they came. I could use this section to share stories from my life about how the goodness and mercy of the Lord saved me from so many things. But instead, just keep reading and you will see more of my testimonies throughout the book. I'm sure you'll be amazed and as I said before, if He'll do it for me, He can certainly do it for you. I challenge you to tap into your circumstances and see just how He has brought you through, time and time again.

You must always open your heart and mind to endless possibilities each day. So many times we miss out on things because of our limited thinking. One of the first things we must do is change our way of thinking. We would be surprised at the things that are waiting for us if we simply open ourselves to receive. One must also understand how powerful the universe is, and its ability to bring exactly what we need at the very moment we need it. There have been so many times when I wasn't sure how I was going to do something, or how a bill was going to be paid, or how I would even make a meal for my children. The only thing I was sure of, is that I would trust in the Lord to make a way out of no way. Time after time He did and always will.

You see, I understand that through faith, God is my source of everything. When I was weak, He was my strength. When I was sick, He was my healer; when I was broke He was, and is, my provider. I think you get where I'm going. When I think of His goodness, all I can do is say - thank you Lord.

When considering new possibilities we must observe all aspects of our lives that encourage negative habits or beliefs. Then we have to let them go. When we release them, we deny their influence. Part of opening the door to new opportunities means we must make a choice. We can surround ourselves with people who are interested in moving to another level and those who are willing to celebrate our accomplishments, as we achieve them.

We must always consider the infinite possibilities and open our hearts and minds to receive them. God gives us unlimited resources that we may tap into at any time. We must wake up each day with great expectations. Each day I expect to be fixed, full and whole. Wholeness can come in an instant, if you just have faith and believe. Some people who have experienced brokenness over their lifetime may not even feel wholeness is possible. To that I say - stop lying to yourself, and realize that going through is only a testament of your faith.

6.

Worth Saving

"It is never too late to be what you might have been."
- George Eliot

I am so glad that while battling breast cancer, God saw that my life was worth saving! I am excited about my testimony, and even more excited about the opportunity to share it with the world. When He has been so good, you simply cannot take it for granted. You must be a witness of His goodness and grace. Often times when sharing my story I tell people that cancer was only the tip of the iceberg. This trial often gets the attention of people because so many people have been impacted by cancer in one way or another. It is usually not a positive experience, but I will tell you, throughout this book you must turn a negative into a positive. It is all about your mindset.

I am so glad I am finally diving in head first as it relates to maximizing my potential and taking the opportunity to share my gifts with multitudes of people. I want to simply empty what's been deposited in me – the gift of motivation. I have experienced the gift from both sides, I have been given wisdom and I have shared wisdom with others. Wisdom is a gift that is absolutely priceless. We all have so much to learn from one another. I have had personal mentors and mentors from afar. One of the greatest losses in the world is when you lose a mentor. They are so valuable, you feel as if you can never gain enough knowledge from them. This is another personal motivation of mine; I want the words of this book to be uplifting to people long after I have departed from this earth. We all have an expiration date, but our legacy can live on in books.

The sad part about it is, our youth have gotten so far away from reading they miss out on tons of blessings and guidance. When I was younger I didn't understand why folks used to tell us how important it was to read the Bible. There is so much information in it. It is truly a step-by-step, how-to guide to life. It tells us about the creation of the earth, the purpose of marriage, the way to overcome challenges, what we were designed to do, what the purpose of the enemy is, and it also includes 7000 promises. The Bible is absolutely awesome. I encourage you to explore it; in case you have not. I can promise that you'll find the answers to some of the problems you have been facing. Not only will you get the answers to some, if not all, of your problems, but you may also discover the purpose for your life; your destiny will be revealed.

Don't ever underestimate your value. You are a masterpiece, there will never be another one like you. You are perfect; being you. Never look at someone else and attempt to duplicate their style. That is commonplace these days. People are always looking at what someone else has and trying to figure out how to get it. We never know what a person had to go through or sacrifice to get what they have. Often times, the grass looks greener on the other side, when you get up close you realize you should've stayed and watered your own grass.

To share a real life example of this theory; there was a married couple where the wife had to have a hysterectomy. Because of it, the husband wanted to get a divorce. Once he got a divorce and remarried another woman, one that he considered to be perfect, he discovered that she also had a hysterectomy 20 years prior, talk about feeling like an idiot! I'll bet he did. Sometimes it is better to stay the course. I also think that God has a sense of humor and I love Him for that.

Don't settle for less than you deserve, if something is less than what you expected it to be, never sell yourself short. When you set your eye on a prize, stand firm and don't be moved by anything you see. Many times we work jobs that pay us less than we are worth and we continue to work for them day after day. Unfortunately we don't say anything, but it is important to speak up because if we don't that company or employer certainly won't. As a matter of fact most employers will take advantage of your worth and do as much as possible to get as much work out of you, for the least cost. How can we expect anyone to know our value, if we don't know our value?

This is not just true in relationships with our employers but in personal relationships as well. I'd like to share a personal testimony that occurred during the process of writing this book. I experienced a few trials when it came to relationships but I never settled for less than I deserved. I knew what I wanted so I put it in writing back in 2009 and there was nothing that would stop me from obtaining the man I wanted. Not even cancer, not the loss of my breast, nor any of the scars on my body. There were many days that I stepped out of the shower and looked at my scars and said, "I am going to be married one day and my husband will love me in spite of my scars". I realize that although I've been battered and bruised from the journey, I'm still alive, in the land of the living and I still have a lot of life to live. Life goes on.

I am glad throughout my struggles no matter the test or how hard the road may seem, I will never give up because good things come to those who wait. When we are in the waiting period we must have the faith to believe there is someone out there designed especially for us. I have had a lot of practice along the way and I can admit that I've met some devils. There have been many times I met guys of whom I thought,

"This is the one for sure!" But none were anywhere near equipped with the qualities I deserved.

They certainly didn't have what I desired in a man. I pulled out my list and they did not measure up. I should have known they would end up being a waste of time, but I often tried to make the shoe fit, even when I knew it was two sizes too small. Although we often use the phrase "Let go and let God", it is much easier said than done. How many times have you given something to your source in prayer and confession, but you just couldn't leave it there? We have often asked our source to deal with it, yet we can't keep our hands off of it. We must learn to rest in our source and believe that He has our best interest at heart. We must understand that He is not going to wrestle with us for control over our issues.

If you, like me, are in a waiting period and you made poor choices, learn from those experiences and mistakes. After all, as the old saying goes, "A mistake is only a mistake if you don't learn from it." This is why I say don't be ashamed of your life story. Your trials purposely propel you into your destiny. Nothing happens by surprise, it all has its purpose. Every dead end relationship was supposed to teach you something. Every person that left your life was supposed to leave at the very moment they left. Every person that came across your path came for a season and once the season was complete, no matter how difficult it was to let them go, understand, it was time.

7.

When the Answer is NO!

"Faith is about trusting God when you have unanswered questions."
- Joel Osteen

Sometimes we feel as if we are going through too much and we ask God to lighten the load and He says no. The reason He says no is because He knows that His grace is sufficient and He gives us the stamina to run the race. That's why He trusts us with trouble. Our obstacles build our character by giving us tenacity, glory, blessing, wisdom, power, fight, drive and motivation. God will be glorified by our test and trials and how we respond to them. We must go from worry to worship. We have to trust God in all situations.

The word No can be positive! Many times we ask for things we truly don't want or are not ready to receive. For example, some people ask for a financial blessing of overflow, but when they receive it they are, honestly, just not ready. Some people prove they are not ready for a large financial blessing because when they receive a small amount they are not good stewards over it (careless spending). If God can trust you with the little, then He knows He can trust you to be faithful with a large quantity of cash. When we are given a small amount of something and we are responsible with it, then we know have passed the test!

There are others with a strong desire to be in a relationship and they want love, but they don't love themselves. You must love and appreciate yourself before God will allow that special person to come into your life. So often we ask for a relationship and either nothing happens or we meet everything except the perfect one God has for us. People often get discouraged during the waiting period and feel that waiting is an obstacle, but truly that is the time we need to be perfecting ourselves for our soulmate. When God says no to relationships, especially those that we should not be connected to, He is attempting to produce perseverance, character and hope in us.

God desires to give us His very best, and if that means saying no to something we desire right now, we just have to trust His timing. I have discovered that when He says no, we simply have to rejoice and be glad that He is not ready for us to have that particular thing at that particular time. He is pleased with His children when we have an attitude of gratitude. We must rest in the fact that although He doesn't always give us what we want, He knows exactly what we need.

While celebrating when God tells us no, we should also be asking for open doors. Open doors lead us into a deeper, more meaningful relationship with God. When we ask for open doors, we are asking Him to open the doors to His will for our lives. At times, we tend to become discouraged when we pray for something and our prayer is not answered the way we feel it should be. We should be happy that He blocks that obstacle, because after all, what God has for us is for us! When He says no, often times that leads us to a righteous path and scripture says, "...the steps of a good man are ordered by the Lord, and he delights in his way". (Psalms 37:23)

When the answer is no, we must keep in mind that what looks good is not always good for us. One of the greatest lessons I am trying to share is, we must simply trust God and His timing, in all things. God's delay does not mean denial. We must realize that sometimes God says no to things because of the sin that is in our lives. We have the potential to delay things when we do not walk according to His will. I would caution you against becoming upset with God and I would encourage you to be thankful in all things. Maintain that attitude of gratitude. Close your eyes and take the time to reflect on the things that you have asked for and He said no to, He is so faithful even when we are not.

As mentioned before, after receiving my bachelor's degree I applied for over 200 jobs and consistently heard the word no or nothing at all. But I never gave up. I changed my focus. Instead of applying for jobs I've come to realize that God wants me to do something greater and maybe He wants me to be my own boss. That way, I can be a blessing to others who have experienced the same rejection I had. Being told no, time and time again, could have really frustrated me; but instead I chose to press on. That is exactly what the enemy wants you to do, he wants you to get frustrated and give up. When you feel that way, I urge you not to quit. This is where faith comes in, the faith to believe that all things are possible. When you feel the strong desire to quit tell yourself, "This is only a test" then ask yourself, "Will I pass or fail?"

It can truly be a blessing to be told no, because it causes us to look deeper within ourselves and figure out who we really are and discover what it is we want out of life. I can honestly say, I now understand that being told no on all those jobs was because they were not the job for me. It is like, none of those jobs would've fueled my passion for people and if I had gotten one of them, it is highly likely I would not have been happy. I probably would not have fulfilled my purpose in writing this book. I am so thankful for every single "no" because I am walking into my purpose with grace and favor! Please don't be dismayed when you hear that word, just consider the fact that you might have been headed in the wrong direction. Sometimes, when we are waiting for God to move an obstacle, He may be waiting for us to let some things go. In order for us to be blessed and to walk into our purpose, we need to let go of some things. Some of these things could be people, TV shows, smoking, drinking, clubbing, cursing, and video game playing and anything else that is not pleasing in the eyesight of God.

8.

Overcoming Life's Obstacles

"It always seems impossible until it is done."
-Nelson Mandela

Definition of obstacle: a thing that blocks ones way, prevents or hinders progress.

Synonyms for obstacle: barrier, hurdle, stumbling block, obstruction, bar, black, impediment, hindrance, snag, cat, drawback, hitch, handicap, deterrent, complication, difficulty, problems, disadvantage, curb, check, monkey wrench, jam, occlusion, blockage.

Don't ever be discouraged because we all have to go through things from time to time. Our obstacles are not designed to block us, they are designed to strengthen us. Life is a journey and some of our dreams take a lifetime to achieve. No matter where we are in our journey, we must not give up. When everything in us tells us to quit, that is when we must work harder. So that means, if you start something - finish it. If you begin working on a book, complete it because somebody needs to read it. If you are a songwriter, write that song because the radio is waiting to play it over and over and over again (and you get royalties each time it is played).

If you are great at fixing things, someone is waiting to have something fixed. If you are an artist draw a picture, there's somebody waiting to buy it. If you are a motivational speaker start preparing your speeches and get ready to travel the world. I could go on and on. Just know, the world is waiting for you; it needs your gifts and talents. Since you now know that the world is waiting for you - please don't give up on your passion. When you walk away from your dreams consider the source and ask yourself "Why am I walking away?"

Are you walking away because someone said you were not good enough to do what God has put on your heart to do? Are you walking away from your dreams because you feel like it's not happening fast enough? If so, I urge you to keep going. Your breakthrough could happen tomorrow; the day after you gave up, your breakthrough could've been waiting for you.

Are you giving up on your dreams because you don't believe God hears your prayers? I want to assure you that He does, loud and clear. However, we must accept that it may not be our season to grow in that area. When we feel like we are ready for something,

God knows better because He knows us. If it is not happening on your timetable, I encourage you to simply be patient and wait on God. When you're facing an obstacle, steady yourself, your mind. Focus and tell yourself, "I am going to get through this; there is victory on the other side!" Focus less on the obstacle and more on what you are supposed to learn while going through your waiting period.

Are you feeling overwhelmed? Don't be dismayed, that very issue you are facing right now, so many others have conquered it. If they can do it so can you! I felt the need to share this because when you are facing certain situations the world can feel like a lonely place. I want you to know that you are never alone, God is always with you. The Bible tells us that we will have troubles, but we have to believe that He is greater than every issue that comes our way. This is encouraging news because we can still be in trouble and simply put our faith in Him to handle every obstacle that tries to block us from our rightful place.

Some obstacles seem like impossible tasks, but nothing is impossible with God. I tell people all the time to dream big because I strongly believe that God wants us to trust Him to do the miraculous. And when we trust Him, He can give us His best. I believe that He wants to show us His mighty acts of grace, mercy and blessings. Since God can part the seas or feed 5000 people with two fish and five loafs of bread or heal the woman with the issue a blood; who bled for

12 years, is there anything we can ask that is too hard for Him? He allows breakthroughs to occur in our lives because we already know that He can do whatever He chooses whenever He chooses.

We all have challenges that we must overcome. You don't have to invite them, they just have a way of showing up; especially at times when you are not ready. God allows obstacles because they help develop us or simply prepare us for future assignments. Sometimes He allows us to go through obstacles so that He may be glorified. He will allow us to experience a test in order to be a testimony in the eyes of others. He will allow the test and testimony to occur while you have witnesses watching by the masses (social media for example).

Are you frustrated by your obstacles? If so, I am glad that you are reading this book because it was written just for you. If that is not you, just keep reading because obstacles will come your way, I promise you. There is no way around them, you must simply overcome them! Some children are born into obstacles, like drug addicted babies, or babies who are born into homelessness, or those born with disabilities. Most of us cannot imagine what that feels like, which is something to be thankful for. When you discover that someone else is experiencing obstacles in their life, you should lend a helping hand if at all possible. You will be pleasantly surprised to know that if you help someone else in their time of trouble, favor will be returned to you at the exact moment you

need it. We all need help from time to time, ev
we think we don't, we do. Most times when you ⌐
going through something, it just makes it easier when
you know you are not alone.

At times, when we go through challenges, they
cause you to be elevated to a new level. My
assignment is to tell you, when it looks like you are
facing a dilemma, or you feel like your back is against
the wall; there is more fight in you. Please don't give
up or give in because your best days are around the
corner. Just on the other side of the wall your back is
up against, is your breakthrough. It may not feel like it
when you're going through, but if you give your best,
despite your circumstances, you will be amazed at the
progress you will make.

No matter what you're going through, put your
best foot forward and stop making excuses. That will
make whatever you do prosper, just keep your chin
up. This is important to reinforce because often times
the things we go through can cause us to be bitter.
That is the time we must keep our minds focused on
the prize. The message throughout this book is not
about what we have to go through in life, instead it's
the way we choose to respond to those challenges. I
can't emphasize enough how important it is to keep
an attitude of gratitude, because these are all life
lessons we must learn from. Life's obstacles tend to be
great teachers. We must be mindful that they have a
greater purpose than what we see going on in the
natural. If we maintain a good attitude, while also

realizing that the storms come to propel us into our destiny, we will have a much better attitude while withstanding the rain. I have learned during my trials, to have a great expectation of restoration when the trial ends.

I have discovered that we should not be upset with people we feel have done us wrong, instead we should realize that God used them as a vessel, or an agent, to get us to the place He wanted us to be. Having a forgiving heart is an obstacle for a lot of people. If it were not for my obstacles in life I would not have written this book! Give thanks for every obstacle, because they truly have a purpose. The devil might have meant it for our bad, but God will turn it around for our good. If I had not gone through obstacles I would still be going to work at a job that literally made me sick. It is so hard to understand things when you're going through a rough patch, but when you realize it is all part of a greater plan, you can't help but be filled with joy. I understand it now, and you will too; if it were not for your experiences you would not be the awesome person that you are today.

Focus on what you can do, not on what you can't. Never use obstacles as an excuse, we all have obstacles to overcome. Some will be tougher than others and some will add heartache and pain, but don't allow the pain to cause you to be bitter. Never surrender and never be afraid to be yourself. Be creative, embrace rejection. Obstacles sometimes give you no other option. Attitude is everything, don't quit, stand up for what you believe in. There is beauty on the inside of you. The unknown is waiting for you to step up and step out.

Change your mindset. Don't give up, now is not the time – never is it time to give up. So many times you've been, oh so close to success but you gave up. You see, everyone has the ability to win with the right attitude. We must travel through life believing that, the rest of our life, has the ability to be the best of our lives.

What do you do when you cannot control your circumstances? You must change your attitude about it. Don't be afraid to ask for help. As a matter fact, you'll be surprised to see how God has placed people in your path to assist you. It is not about what happens to you in life, it's all about how you respond to it. Doing nothing is not an option. When obstacles come you must take action to overcome them.

An obstacle can be like a brick wall, the question is, "Are you willing to tear it down?" Some obstacles are only obstacles because they are unfamiliar to us. Uncertainty can cause fear. When fear arises, that's when you should step into the unknown. Often, when you play it safe you miss out on so much. For example, some people drive the same brand of car because that's all they have ever known, and they eat the same food when they go to restaurants because they are afraid of trying something new. They shop at the same stores because they are familiar with them.

We live in a world where there is so much to explore, we can't imagine how much we are actually missing out on. I challenge you to live each day like it is your last. Do something that you've never done.

Your words reveal what's on the inside of you. If you want to be noticed as outstanding in your field, one yes is all you need. Get outside of your own mental walls. Don't see things the way others see them. Go beyond your barriers, enlarge your territory and you will change in every area in your life. Prayer works and it also changes things always be alert for unexpected blessings, because they are on the way!

9.

Hidden Obstacles

"What you do today will improve all your tomorrows."
- Ralph Marston

Hidden obstacles can come in the form of unfulfilling jobs, toxic friends, poor time management and goals that have no purpose. These are the obstacles that are right in front of you, but are not obvious. Once they are revealed and removed, there is no doubt you will become successful and feel a renewed sense of happiness. Dead end meaningless jobs can make you feel like a slave. So many people don't understand why they feel such a sense of relief when they are no longer with a company. It should be obvious, it's because they were not supposed to be there anyway.

Some people feel a sense of relief when certain friendships and relationships end because those relationships drain the life from you. Perhaps you were not supposed to be there and/or your season with them was over. Remember, each person that comes in your life is either a blessing or a lesson. Sometimes, after you discover the lesson it is time to move on.

The obstacle of poor time management is simply put "the ghost of wasting time." We are all guilty of wasting time. It could be something as simple as procrastinating when you know you should be doing something. I can honestly say that when I was writing this, I was really eager to get this book published. But there were times when I was at home lying in bed, knowing full well that I should be writing in order to bring this project to a close. The point you should take away is the fact that when you waste time, you delay your destiny. Time is something that we should not take for granted and it should be used wisely. Your destiny is waiting for you so be motivated to do all you can and be all that you can be. Time is precious and should not be wasted. Please stop procrastinating, and go after your dreams. Don't waste another moment, because time is NOT on your side. The world needs your talent, never forget - your talent was meant to be shared with the world!

When goal setting, make it a priority to set goals that help you chip away at your ultimate goal for success in life. Some folks make goals that serve no purpose at all, similar to taking a detour instead of a straight path down the road of least resistance. Make life easy for yourself, don't take detours to your destiny. Get there as fast as you can, without delay. You have been waiting long enough.

Enjoy the Journey!

*"Hardships often prepare ordinary people
for extraordinary destiny."*
- *CS Lewis.*

Your journey starts today, don't wait until tomorrow. Do what you want to do today. We have an unlimited number of opportunities each day. Never settle, always dare to be different, don't fit into black-and-white scenario. Don't be mediocre. Believe in yourself. Trust in your abilities. Know that if you follow the crowd you will get lost in it. Understand that no one has smooth sailing all the time. Trials will come and being angry about them is simply a waste of time.

More often than not we need to simply surrender everything and fully trust God. We don't need to know all the details, we simply need to be confident in the fact that the right outcome will unfold. When we turn our obstacles over to Him, stress should be released immediately. We have to take our hands off the challenges we face and simply believe.

It's all right to be frustrated and discouraged

sometimes, however, it is not ok to stay there. You may participate in self-pity, but only for a little while. If you stay in this type of mindset for too long, you may make the wrong decisions. When you are in a funk, that's usually when you look at the lives of others and it looks like they are winning and accomplishing their goals. At the same time you may feel that you've been praying to God and your prayers have gone unanswered. When you feel this way, it is time to celebrate those around you who are walking into their seasons of purpose and destiny instead of being jealous of them. Being jealous of others, who have waited their turn, is a way to block your blessings and cause your purpose and destiny to be put off even further. It is so easy to look at another person's life, yet not understand all they had to suffer through to get to their place of glory.

Some people make the fatal mistake of comparing their lives to others, then feel unfulfilled in their own lives. Comparing our lives to the lives of others can be detrimental. The reason is because we don't know someone else's story of triumph. We may never know how many celebrities, now in the limelight, have had their own struggles with thoughts of suicide. Speaking of suicide it is important to mention that **suicide is a permanent solution to a temporary problem**. It is certainly food for thought and something you should share with someone who may be struggling with thoughts of suicide.

Once you realize you have a bright future ahead of

you, rest assured, the going gets tough sometimes; but you can persevere. You still have a long road to travel before you arrive at your destiny. It is also noteworthy to mention that getting a blessing too soon is not a blessing at all. God knows when you are ready to be blessed! We are being taught patience on the journey. No matter what our desires are, ultimately God's will, will be done. Before we were formed, our destinies were already prepared; but often times our choices and unwillingness to be patient must be sacrificed.

Change Your Mindset

*"Your attitude, not your aptitude,
will determine your altitude."*
- Zig Ziglar

How many things have you allowed to destroy you because of your mindset? A lot of times we are our own worst enemy by the thoughts we keep. It's possible to become prisoners of our own minds when the thoughts we have hold us captive. Once you discover the origin of your fears it is time you eliminate them all from your mind. The mind is such a powerful tool, so you must first overcome fear; the rest is easy. It's the exact same way for worrying. When we worry about something, it means we don't trust God, according to the word of God. (Matthew 6:30) Worry is anxiety over potential or actual problems. Many times people worry about potential issues that may never materialize. That worry can be classified as a total waste of time.

Fear and worrying can totally dominate our

thoughts, but we don't have to let them. When negative thoughts pop into our minds we have to take control of them and ask ourselves why are we worrying or why do we have this nagging feeling of fear. Then we must ask ourselves "How is this going to help the situation?" There is no purpose for it unless it's going to drive you to make positive changes, such as changing your diet to reduce the opportunity for the recurrence of cancer. I use this example because so many people have no idea that a poor diet can contribute to a diagnosis of cancer. The fear of being alone could cause someone to change their attitudes about relationships. The fear of sexually transmitted diseases may cause people to move away from premarital sex. The fear of drowning may cause someone else to take swimming lessons. The point that I am trying to drive home is, not all fear is bad.

If you change the way you think about it, you can use fear to your advantage. We should all do our very best to turn a negative situation into a positive one. That will give you power over all situations. Again, I remind you that your mindset is a powerful tool. When facing challenges, we must learn to look at them from several different angles. Many times people fail to reach their goals and dreams because they suffer from limited thinking and allow fear to paralyze them.

Limited thinking can be a hindrance to success. One of the first things that comes to mind is people who live in impoverished communities. Their thinking is so limited they cannot see a way out. If I cannot show them there is so much more to life that cannot be seen, my purpose in writing this book would be lost.

<u>SIDEBAR:</u> That's another reason it is so important to read books, not only this one, but books in general. They provide so much insight, but technology has changed the way our young people, adults too, are missing out on what's on the inside of books. With technology in our hands, we have so much knowledge at our fingertips, but we are often not willing to explore it. We would much rather hang out on social media and gaming sites. If only we would use these tools to explore wisdom and knowledge, the world will be a much better place.

Begin to have a mindset of forgiveness for those who have hurt you. That's the point of taking on His likeness - God is a forgiving God. We often hold onto grudges against others, yet we want God to forgive us when we fall short of His will. That doesn't make sense. Are you holding on to unforgiveness in your heart against someone who hurt you? That lack of forgiveness could be a barrier to you overcoming obstacles that you face right now.

Turn obstacles into opportunities! Anytime you face obstacles try to find the positive in it. Don't ever allow it to discourage you, words are powerful. Words can give life or cause death. Money cannot heal the soul. Don't look for love in all the wrong places. Positive thinking helps to promote the ability to overcome adversity and difficulties in life. It is imperative to adopt the attitude of positive thinking no matter your situation or circumstance. Adopt it and believe in it with your heart and soul.

Have confidence in yourself! If you have confidence in yourself, you'll begin to believe that you can achieve whatever your heart desires. Your attitude can attract both positive and negative things. It is up to you, what will you choose? When you wake up in the morning do you choose happiness or sadness? I hope your answer is that you choose happiness. If not, I encourage you to wake up with a great expectation each morning!

You can envision your life in whatever condition you see fit. One fun way to do this is to create a vision board. It is an exciting activity, one that you can create alone, with family, friends, co-workers or your church family. The purpose of a vision board is to be a blank canvas for you to write or attach pictures of the way you envision your life. My current vision board is filled with love, health, finances, travel, wealth, marriage, family and of course God. I keep it at home in a place where I see it most of the day. It is a constant reminder of what my life will become. I know that the best days of my life are ahead of me and I look forward to checking off the visions on my board; one by one. Now, this is an illustration of what my vision board consists of, but yours is just that, "yours".

And it is up to you to make it specific to your desires.

Let's spend more time on vision boards and discuss how they can be helpful to you. What we focus on expands, so once you complete your vision board and put it in a place where you see it daily, you unconsciously do visualization exercises. Vision boards force you to focus on what you want into your life. They also bring your visions to life. Visualizing can cause happy thoughts to occur in the same way the horrific things that are happening in the world and on the news, cause us to feel depressed and sad. We have to consistently surround ourselves with things and people who inspire us.

I want you to feel inspired and be motivated to be the very best version of yourself possible, because you are significant. While reading this book, be sure to create a vision board and understand that there are no limits, there is no wrong way to go about it, just do it!

Be determined to change your mindset, let your actions speak louder than your words. There was a time it nearly burned my ears to hear people say "I am a Christian". This should never have to be announced because your actions should demonstrate the obvious.

Words have so much power. We must take inventory of what we say because we speak words over our lives every day. When we face planned or unplanned obstacles, we must speak victory over them. If it's a dark situation, we need to speak light over it, if it's sickness, we need to talk about health and healing. If the issue is lack of resources, we must speak abundance. For each problem we face, God is the source of every solution. Obstacles are like storms or traffic jams, they eventually clear, you just have to believe and be patient.

We must always focus on the positive in every situation because whatever we focus on is magnified. This is why I focused on God and healing when I was going to treatment for cancer. We truly become what we think. If we constantly focus on our problems, or being defeated in one area or another, it not only becomes magnified in our lives, but the negativity drains us. Speak over your life words that are uplifting and edifying, not only for yourself, but also for those around you.

It is important to be connected to others because we all need someone else at one time or another. We were not designed to act alone. Being connected to others does not mean you'll always be in a place of agreement with them. However, there is a blessing in our differences. This would be a boring place if we were all on the same page and shared the same thoughts. Every person around you should bring value to you and you should bring value to them as well. If the people around you are not adding value, it is time to disconnect from that negative source of energy.

Negative sources drain your personal resources and can become an obstacle in your life. They influence your thinking. For example, a child growing up in a household with parents who constantly tell them they are dumb, stupid, crazy or will never amount to anything, well, the child will begin to believe those words. They will haphazardly begin to live up to what's been said about them. It is vital to speak affirmations over their lives and teach them to do the same for themselves at an early age. Some examples of positive affirmations for children include, but are not limited to:

- You are limitless,
- You can achieve anything,
- Never give up,
- You are smart,
- You are capable,
- You are beautiful,
- Choose to be happy,
- You are blessed,
- You are a great leader,
- You are successful,
- Believe in yourself

There will be a stark difference between children who are given negative energy, versus those who are showered with positive affirmations. No matter what words you speak over yourself or your children, always remember, these words will take shape. Which words have you chosen to speak over your life? How will that change after reading this book? The choice is yours and has always been. You have the power!

The Company You Keep

*"All our dreams can come true,
if we have the courage to pursue them."*
– Walt Disney

Toxic people can be hard to ignore – just do your best! Anyone who doesn't support your dreams and aspirations and is full of negativity can be considered toxic. These negative people will also dismiss any attempts for you to better yourself. That may be because they don't have any goals and they are threatened by someone who does. Often this person is afraid that you would pull away from them if you begin to better yourself. The fact is that we all want to have friends, but we would never imagine that our friends would be the ones holding us back from being great.

We need to connect with people who drive us to success, folks that question our level of growth. We need to associate ourselves with people who are driven. When you associate yourself with highly motivated individuals, they give you the support you need when times get tough and those unexpected obstacles arise. People who are motivated tend to find the positive in every situation and encourage you to dust yourself off and get back on task. When engaging with the highly motivated, there is always a little friendly competition going on. Lesson to the wise, if your inner circle of friends doesn't motivate you, you need to make some changes. Don't limit yourself, there are resources out there and groups waiting for you to join them. Together you can be great.

I remember back when I was working at a small community hospital, just being around doctors and nurses and other professionals made me want to elevate my status. A more specific example is when I was considering going back to school to work on my bachelor's degree. I was ready to move full speed ahead until it was time to discuss payment options for college. I was paralyzed with fear when the financial aid advisor talked about taking out student loans. Thankfully, after my conversation with the advisor, there was a coworker nearby that I talked to about the dilemma I was facing. He assured me that one of the best investments I could make was in me. And after putting things in perspective, it was no longer difficult for me to make the decision. If we don't invest in ourselves, how do we expect anyone else to?

I was thankful to have someone with that mindset in close proximity; I could've easily been in the presence of naysayers. They would've alternately stated, "Oh you don't need to go to school, there's no future in education - all they want is your money." It is often said that the universe/God will send you what or who you need to accomplish your dreams, goals and visions. I can attest to this truth because there were so many times I worked on projects and God sent someone to assist me when I needed help. I can say that a simple conversation with my coworker is part of the reason I hold the degrees that I have today. I wish there was a way I could say thank you but I don't think I will ever see him again and I couldn't tell you what his name was if I tried. This is why it is so important to speak positively in the lives of others, because you never know the effect it will have on the person you are speaking with. Then you can pay it forward.

People often say you become like those you spend your time with, and instantly I think, "I need to find some millionaires to hang out with! People with extremely positive mindsets". The truth is, I actually believe anything is possible. The people we allow to be around us have a great deal of influence on our lives and decisions. This is why the people in our inner circle should be purpose pushers and we should push all others outside of our inner circle. It is imperative to our success that we keep naysayers at a distance because they can become a distraction to our purpose. You can still love them, but from a distance. I remember when I was going to college, whenever I spoke with my biological mom she would say "I don't know why you going to school because there are people out there with PhD's who are stocking grocery shelves." She was basically insinuating that there was no purpose in going to school. What a dream killer! Although, she was negative, I took the opportunity to turn that negative into a positive by making sure I support my children in the things they are passionate about. Additionally, I never allowed her negativity to stop my progress and I didn't just finish, but I finished strong. I share this life experience because this is my truth and I wanted to demonstrate that no matter the relationship, you cannot allow anyone to destroy the vision you have for your future.

People can have a huge impact on your life, that's why it is important to minimize the number of negative people in your life. Negative people are like poison, they have the ability to drain the happiness from you. They complain all the time and usually have something negative to say about everything. It is a good idea to counter everything a negative person says with something positive, be their ray of sunshine anytime you come in contact with them.

Furthermore, because people can have such a huge impact, you must be careful who you allow to be in your presence. I often tell people that the company you keep speaks volumes about who you are. Negative people often seek out other negative people so they can engage in negative conversation. If this is you, step outside of your comfort zone and experience people who are different from you.

Let me share some helpful hints, tools that you can use when it comes to improving your inner circle. Reduce the negativity - unfortunately the world we live in thrives off negativity because it sells everything better. For example, take a look at the movies that are most popular, the music that promotes negativity and, last but not least, consider what you see on the news and in social media. On just about every hand there is no shortage of negativity. Even in your close personal relationships, nearly every person you talk to is eager to share their negative experiences. Now, please understand, I am not telling you not to support those who are close to you. We all need to vent once in a while, but what I am saying is, keep it to a minimum. When you care about someone, it is easy to make their problems your own. It has been my suggestion that if you have issues, talk to your source (God) about them, He is the only one that can change what you are going through. We could never imagine how much stress we place on someone else who likely has enough issues of their own to deal with. Of course there will be people who need you at times, and then there are others who are always a complete drain on your energy. By the way, that can be detrimental to your health.

Your success can often be defined by the people you choose to spend time with. You should make a valiant effort to interact with the people who mean the most to you. Life is too short to waste time on anything. Be mindful to surround yourself with good people. Good people are positive, happy and upbeat. Seek out people who inspire you to be a better you and also those who motivate you. Your inner circle should encourage you to feel confident; they should support your causes. They should also have the ability to make you feel happy and energized. It is my opinion that the energy of the people you surround yourself with should be contagious. Therefore individuals who emit negative energy, bring about stress, or add drama to your life, it would be wise to keep your contact with them to a minimum.

When determining who you want in your circle, you should complete a self-evaluation exercise to figure out what type of person you are; after all, like attracts like. If you treat people well and exude confidence, it will lead you down a path to meet more people like that. Make a commitment to yourself to surround yourself with people who are good to you and treat you the way you desire to be treated.

Choices

"God always gives His best to those who leave the choice with Him."
- Jim Elliot

Each day we have a number of choices we make, from the time we wake up, until the time we go to sleep. Many of the decisions we make are done without thought. I challenge you to be intentional as you go about your day and objectively consider each of your decisions. Each decision has consequences. Often we ignore the fact that many decisions we make have a lasting impact on our lives. With that being true it is imperative to live on purpose. Measure the pros and cons of each choice by taking an objective look at the matter at hand.

The choices we make have the ability to set us apart from the crowds. We are all given 86, 400 seconds each day and what we choose to do with them is what makes us uniquely individual. Most people who are successful wake up early in the morning in order to capitalize on each second. It is not uncommon for average people to sleep while those who excel in life are maximizing their potential. Insomniacs are some of the most creative people, since they can't sleep they often put that time to good use.

Choices are similar to building blocks in our lives. There are times when we are going to make bad choices. When that happens and the consequences of our choices prove to be negative, we learn from that experience. Some have said that experience is the best teacher. I'm sure we could all remember a time when we did something that our parents told us not to and we had to pay the price. On the flip side there have been times when we have made decisions that brought us great joy. When that happens, we want to make those kind of decisions more often. We cannot allow fear to drive us into straying away and missing out on the life God intended for us.

Be bold! if you want something, go get it! Greater is coming. Make a choice, your choices have power. Decide that you're going to be successful. Decide that you're going to create a great life for yourself. I have decided that if I don't move to motivate people, I am not doing what God placed me on this earth to do. I now know who I am and why I was created. And now that I know, I have to be committed to my purpose. I want to motivate people every day. I want my words to inspire you to be the best at whatever your purpose, talents, or gifts are. I want to encourage you to excel in your craft. I want to inspire you to be dedicated to your purpose, once you have identified what it is.

Our choices in life demonstrate the amount of power we have in any given situation. Therefore, the more we know, the better we are. There is an old saying, "knowledge is power" and it is so true, but the Bible says it differently. It says, people are destroyed for lack of knowledge. (Hosea 4:6) When we lack knowledge, which we all do in certain areas, it is easy for us to be taken advantage of. This is the reason it is important to use technology in ways that enhance our knowledge. Often times we use things that could help us in the wrong manner, things meant for our good can sometimes be the very things to destroy us. For example, texting is a great tool for communicating information quickly, but it also can be deadly if used while driving. It is critical to use your discretion about things that could help or hurt. Facebook (and social media) is another method of communication. It could be great for allowing family and friends to keep in contact, but if used recklessly, it can cause people to be killed over information that has been displayed there.

The choices we make in life are critical to our success or demise. For example, let's look at the life of a 27 year old football player who, just four years before taking his own life, was awarded a 40 million dollar contract. The very year that he signed the contract, he made a decision to take the life of someone else. That choice cost him his life in more ways than one. He was not only cut from the team, but he was convicted of murder and was sentenced to life in prison. This young man had a chance to appeal his sentence which could have possibly led to his release from prison or a reduced sentence; instead he made a choice to take his life. When we are faced with dilemmas it is easy to feel like our choices are limited. More than likely it is our thinking that is limited. It is easy to be narrow-minded versus thinking objectively.

Be Inspired

"Problems in life are like traffic jams.
They eventually clear."
– Malissa Stringer

Never be ashamed of your story, it could motivate others. You'd be surprised to discover how your wounds can turn into wisdom and inspire others to press on when they feel like throwing in the towel. Tell your story without reservation, and watch how He causes others to be blown away by your experiences. As a matter fact, you may find that the broken pieces of your life fit perfectly with someone else's, and is just enough to make each other whole. In order for this to happen, one must realize that in life, you don't look for the one who is perfect. You simply find the one who is perfect for you. He or she is out there, and I encourage you not to give up seeking a successful relationship. I like to remind myself that during the waiting stage, I was being prepared for my mate, and he was being prepared for me. I have had some experiences and some obstacles along the way, but those experiences came into my life to make me better. Each day without him here next to me, allowed me to wake up and declare that I am one day closer to his perfect love. Love is possible, perfection cannot be rushed!

Nobody escapes life's challenges. Every person who has experienced victory has been a victim in some area of their lives. Everyone has a story they might not share with the world, but we all go through things. That's the reason it is important to share our scars with others so they can see that we have been through something and they can feel more confident about what they may be facing. It is so easy to feel as if you are the only person who has ever been through what you are going through. But you're not, I promise.

Know that you can win! You are no different from other successful people. We all have the potential to be great down on the inside of us. We were all born ready! We have to simply tap into our potential and search for the greatness that resides in us because, believe me, it's there. When we read or hear about people who overcame obstacles and arrived at a place of victory, their stories should inspire us to be great. We have to declare that God created us equal and that He is not a respecter of persons. Additionally, when we have a passion to accomplish something, we can't forget that we can do all things through Christ and that we have the ability to do it well. The problem for most of us is limited thinking. We have to focus on changing our minds when it comes to obstacles. Instead of seeing them as barriers, we should look at them as stepping stones.

During my experience as a substitute teacher I would ask the students: "Where are my 4.0 students?" Then I ask: "Where are my 1.8 students?" They usually burst into laughter and I explained that I seriously wanted to know. High school students always come up with crazy, creative answers. After listening to a few responses, I explain that the only difference is potential, and further, we all have it. When I say that it's like a lightbulb went off in their heads as if to say, "Is that all it is?" Yes, for my high schoolers, as well as the person reading this book, I want you to know that you have the potential to be great. You simply have to tap into your ability! The thing that keeps many people from being great is the fact that <u>they are not tapping into their potential</u>.

They allow themselves to be distracted by excessive TV. To be honest, we never have time to watch TV, the junk that comes on today only dumbs us down anyway. Is it the games on your phone that tie up your precious time? Games were a major distraction for me at one time. There was a game on my phone that had me playing it for multiple hours each day until one day I literally woke up. I thought, "This game is robbing me of my precious time that I could be spending with my children, family and friends!" And just like that I gave it up. Often we chase money and never realize that time is our most precious commodity; once it is gone we can never get it back. Each day should be set up like a carefully planned trip to avoid wasting time. It's all about time management; many of the obstacles in life come because we did not plan accordingly. Planning our day helps us maintain accountability in relation to getting the things done that matter most.

In addition to distractions, we need to avoid procrastination. If there is something that needs to get accomplished, we must simply do it without further delay. When we put things off, we tend to do other things that are unintentional time-wasters. This includes social media browsing, checking our emails unnecessarily and talking on the phone, contributing to conversations that are not advancing us. I'd like to explore that last time-waster a little bit deeper, I have a question for you. How many times have you been facing an issue and chose to pick up the phone and tell everyone you could about the issue? As mentioned earlier, it only magnifies the issue instead of resolving it. If this is you, I encourage you to stop it now because that reaction only makes it appear to be greater than it is.

Let's go deeper as it relates to potential. You have so much potential on the inside of you, waiting to be explored. Don't you dare waste another moment on anything other than releasing that potential. It is advised that we write down goals and see how many we can check off in a year's time. We should make our goals far reaching, yet accomplishable; you will be surprised by the things you can do if you only tap into your unused potential. For example, in my household my mom never discussed college because we did not believe we could afford it. Nor did I have the belief that I had the potential to be successful in college. Thankfully I had a mentor who told me and showed me otherwise. She saw my capability even when I did not and that's what I hope to do for you. I want to tell you that it is never too late to accomplish your dreams and aspirations. Whatever you are passionate about, don't waste any more time - start now.

So often I talk to people who have great ideas, inventions and other creative works, but they never choose to share them with the world. They don't realize the financial gain that could result from their ideas. They don't realize how incredibly selfish it is for them to keep it all to themselves when others could benefit from their gifts and talents. I know some people don't tap into their potential because it requires work, but we must realize that anything worth having, is worth working hard for.

We need to recognize that our potential comes from God! It is because of Him that we are equipped with everything we need to be successful. It is pleasing to Him when we tap in and showcase our gifts and talents. When we are in the process of doing this, obstacles come to knock us off track, but we must remain focused. It's when they come that we really have to dig our feet in the sand and discover our true purpose. When obstacles and challenges arise we have the ability to develop a true connection with our Father. There is just something about those times in life when we can't do anything else but depend on Him. It is unfortunate that some people have to go through a crisis to be introduced to God. It is so fulfilling to walk with Him and allow Him to guide you in every area of your life. I am so thankful that I had a relationship with God before the diagnosis of cancer. I can tell you about my experience and challenge you to develop a relationship with Him as soon as possible, if you have not already.

You have the power to be happy in all situations and relationships. Choose to be happy by understanding that the season or the relationship has run its course when it ends. You can also choose happiness when someone has been sick and they pass on. You know they are no longer suffering; that alone is a reason to rejoice. Many times we are sad because we love someone so much that we never want to see them go, even if their quality of life is poor. That's not love, that is pure selfishness and we need to re-evaluate what is important.

Sometimes people find sadness because of the loss of a job, not realizing that when one door closes - another one opens. Many people later discover that the loss of a job is a blessing because it forces them to find their true passion. If people only understood the fact that, when you chase your true passion, most likely, financial gain will follow. Now that I have provided some examples for you, evaluate your life regarding areas in which you can find happiness, by turning a negative into a positive.

15.

Stand Still

"Patience is not simply the ability to wait-
it's how we behave while we're waiting."
— Joyce Meyer

There is a time for everything, so let's discuss the time to stand still. Now, some of you may say that the common theme has been to move, and that is true. But after you have done all that you can do, it is time to be still and let God be God. When we are still, it is the easiest time to hear God's voice.

When we are patient, things fall into place. It is also when ones character is built. I often tell the kids in the classroom, there are no shortcuts when it comes to success or cultivation. That truth is a fact of life. Some things we simply have to go through, there is no easy way around some obstacles. Believe it or not, my patience was tested during the writing of this book. I could hardly wait to finish it so I could share, but I understood that it is a process, and in order for it to be perfected, it was going to take time. I am learning so much through this writing process, it has been totally amazing. We cannot focus on the amount of time something takes to come to fruition. Instead, we must focus on the lesson we are to learn while waiting. The bottom line is - God can change our situation in an instant if He wants to. Many times He doesn't change it because, I believe, He realizes we need to be cultivated in a certain area. This is the reason we have so many tests in life, each of them are designed to develop our spiritual strength.

For example, the relationships people are in prior to marriage should teach us lessons while allowing us to make mistakes. After all, a mistake is only a mistake if we don't learn from it. So, when we are in a relationship and we experience obstacles in that relationship, we should not become angry or give up on it. We should shift our focus to the lesson we are supposed to learn from the experience. This is something that is usually avoided in marriages today because people don't expect to have obstacles, which is insane. Marriage is the union of two imperfect people, who were single, dealing with overcoming obstacles alone. With the union of marriage comes double the obstacles, but the best part about it is you now have someone to work through your obstacles with. That is why you should really get to know the person you plan to marry. You should know how they function under pressure so you're not surprised when you face obstacles together.

While you are standing still and knowing that God

is God, it is a good time to take inventory of the lessons you learn during a given process. Life has a way of teaching us various lessons, but we are not supposed to hide those lessons and keep them to ourselves. We are to share our experiences to help someone else. If I can spare someone else the pain I had to endure, then it is a win-win for everyone involved. We all have life lessons to learn, but if we share some wisdom and insight, the pain for someone else may not be as great. After you have done your part and it's time to stand still, please do not become frustrated when it seems time is not moving fast enough. Just know that His timing is not our timing; but He is never late.

But they that wait upon the LORD shall renew their strength; they shall mount up with wings as eagles; they shall run, and not be weary; and they shall walk, and not faint. Isaiah 40:31

Knowing that everything happens in due time, keeps you from being anxious for anything. It is important not to force something that is not meant to be. For example, most of us living in Michigan, a state where the seasons change, have a favorite season. My favorites are spring and summer. During the winter months, I imagine the trees in full bloom, but I must wait for the seasons to change in the natural. Often times we don't see the joy in waiting, but the appreciation I have when the seasons change is priceless. When we are in the waiting season, there is so much for us to learn. The greatest thing to learn during this time is patience. While in our waiting season, we must find peace. We must also be productive and assist others while waiting for whatever it is we must wait for.

Helping others is priceless. It is an awesome feeling to see someone else achieve their goals. That is my motivation, "The sky is the limit." Waiting patiently is an act of faith. When you know it's coming and you are expectantly waiting, it is easier to wake up each morning. God knows where you are, and how long you've been waiting. We're all in a constant state of waiting for something, but it's all about our attitude while we wait that matters most. There's a saying, "Life is 10% what happens and 90% how we respond to it." It is imperative to have patience in everything, even in relationships, in order for them to be successful. We must be patient while waiting for success. It is a process. Very few processes occur overnight. When we are children, we can't wait to get older, not realizing that being an adult is not all it's cracked up to be. So often I find myself encouraging people to enjoy the season they are in, but we are always so busy trying to get to the next one, that we totally bypass the joys of today.

When we pray for clarity we may never get it. We may never understand His will and that can be a good thing, because we likely would not be able to handle it. If He showed us everything we will encounter, we might begin living recklessly. He wants us to be able to trust Him, by faith. That is one of the reasons we have obstacles, they are places of testing. Although He knows how we are going to resolve our issues before issues arise, more often than not, He will allow trials to last longer based on our response. Therefore, we need to be still while we are going through issues and challenges. Instead of quieting ourselves, we go into a frenzy and then it's difficult to hear Gods voice. It's similar to walking around your home looking for something and you forgot what you were looking for. Usually, you have to go back to the place where you actually had the thought, before you remember what you were searching for. Many times when crisis strikes our lives, we go into panic mode instead of simply asking God, "What do we do now?" Unfortunately, God is often a last resort after we've exhausted all our other options. We would save ourselves a lot of grief if we'd only speak to God first.

Furthermore, we must realize that God sees all. He knows the solution and the multiple alternatives there are to our challenges. We have a tendency to believe there is only one possible solution to our problems. It's that limited thinking which causes us to stress unnecessarily - He's already got it worked out. Our stress is sometimes a result of decisions we have made that brought about the challenge or obstacle we face. With this in mind, it is important to note that not all of life's challenges catch us by surprise. Many of them are self-inflicted which is why we should really think our decisions through before we make them. We understand that children are impulsive by nature, but adults can be extremely impulsive as well. It is often why we find ourselves in situations that could've been otherwise avoided.

Every day we unconsciously make decisions without giving much thought and without realizing the impact of the decision. We are moving so fast that we later ask ourselves "How did that happen?" I encourage you to slow down and evaluate the consequence of a decision before you make it. It really can be the difference between life and death. Often, when we make decisions, we make them under pressure. These decisions can cause you to be taken advantage of depending on who you're dealing with. Never allow someone to rush you into making a decision. You owe it to yourself to think things through and if someone does not allow you the time to make that decision, feel free to decline the offer. Something better must be on its way!

Waiting Season

"Believe you can and you are halfway there."
— Theodore Roosevelt

No one likes to wait, but waiting is often required in life. During the waiting process we are developing. That is why we must not become so focused on what we desire, but on what it takes to get there. While we are in the process of waiting, that is our time to take action and get ready for the blessing. One example we can focus on is marriage, there are so many things one can do to prepare for a marriage. Often times people believe that it takes another to complete them. When entering a marriage, it is important to come to the relationship in wholeness. After speaking with several people on this topic, I am no longer surprised when I hear people say they are broken and they expect relationships to mend that brokenness.

We all have a lot to learn about relationships if we really believe the union of two broken people equals a successful marriage. With this mindset, you have already lost. Waiting for your significant other, is the perfect time to prepare yourself to be an amazing spouse. It is unfortunate that some people waste so much time by idly waiting for an event to happen. There is always something you could be doing while you are in the waiting process. Another common area to highlight is when waiting for what you consider to be the perfect job or career. During this time of waiting, you could be expanding your knowledge base in the area you are seeking to move into. If you are transitioning from one job to another it is important to remain faithful and do the best possible job you can in your current position. It is so easy to become distracted from your current position when you have set your sights on something more appealing. I encourage you to stay focused. You'll find that when you do your best in one situation, opportunities tend to find you. I could go on and on because we are always in a period of waiting, in one area or another, so let's fast forward to your breakthrough!

The waiting season is over and it is time for restoration right now, not later, but right now. God can restore every area of your life. We have to celebrate other people even when we feel He is not answering our prayers. Famine comes sometimes because of sin in our lives, we should take a step back and objectively look at our lives. We need to repent for the things that are not pleasing to God. We must let go of some things He has told us to let go of. We must depend on Him to guide us, but it is up to us to make the changes when we hear His voice. To every season there is a purpose. We must understand that many things occur in life to get you in right relationship with God.

Each day brings new opportunities! Always live, expecting that incredible things will happen at random times. You are talented and you will succeed in life. You are the best of the best. You are indeed an amazing individual, capable of accomplishing your dreams. The only prerequisite is, you must first believe that your dreams are possible!

Perseverance Pays Off

"With a hint of good judgment, to fear nothing, not failure or suffering or even death, indicates that you value life the most. You live to the extreme; you push limits; you spend your time building legacies. Those do not die."
- Criss Jami

When you go through challenges, perseverance is key. You cannot give up. There are so many times people expect you to give up. When you're in a competition and you give up, it makes it easy for all other competitors. Even when there is not a competition, you should consider a race against time or a race against yourself. You want to do what you must to be the best you can possibly be.

Maybe you've been working on something for a long time and you feel it will never come to fruition. Stop thinking negatively. God's delay does not mean denial. It is possible that it has not happened yet, because it is not your season yet. We know that everything has a season. For example, some people want to be married and are not ready yet, they have principles to master before their mate arrives. Sometimes relationships may not work out, not because God does not want it, but because God sees the end before the beginning. He knows the person who is supposed to grow and groom you for your true love. Oftentimes, women get angry when they feel they have groomed a man, then he goes off and marries another woman. That bitterness is mostly self-inflicted. We should not play the role of a wife - before we are actually a wife. The saying goes, "Why buy the cow, when you can have the milk for free?" It is a true statement. Conversely, it happens for men as well. It is much less stated, but pretending to be a husband before commitment is harmful to egos. Men have been hurt when they have been used by a woman; only for that woman to move on to another man.

Another illustration is when you have worked for an employer for years and, after giving it your all, they let you go because they need to reduce costs. Later you find out your position was not eliminated, but filled by someone else, anyone else other than you. The pain from such an event may be hard to put into words, but if you focus on the things that God was trying to show you, you might discover there were warning signs. You would've known that particular assignment was going to end. We must stay alert to changing conditions. Throughout our lives doors close so that new doors can be opened. When one door closes we must stay prepared for the new opportunity to come. I'd like to believe that there are always opportunities around us! The enemy may have meant to harm us, but God allows us to use that situation to our advantage. Always search for the positive in every situation. Although it may not seem like it on the surface, I encourage you to dig deeper. Don't quit, that would be taking the easy way out.

Many people have given up on their dreams and it's sad to see because many times we could be knocking on the door of a blessing and give up. We must be patient even when things don't go the way we thought they should have. True blessings take time; that is not to say things don't change instantly sometimes, but that's not how it usually works. We tend to give up while on the way to victory and we find ourselves in a place of frustration. This is the perfect time to persevere and press on through the temporary pain of our situation. In reality people often make poor decisions out of frustration. If we could only settle ourselves enough to think things through, we would be much more successful. Making decisions in the time of pain, crisis, trials, frustration and even triumph, can be dangerous.

Challenges come to knock you off balance - don't let them. When you look over your life and evaluate the challenges you've faced, you'll be amazed. You'll have to ask yourself, "How did I get through all that trouble?" We will all go through changes and challenges, but every single one of them has a purpose. And if we could just see it for what it is and not feel sorry for ourselves, we may be able to reach our destiny sooner, rather than later.

Sometimes people have to go through things publicly so God can show people that He is bigger than any obstacle one might face. We have to trust Him with every detail of our lives. We must trust Him with the things we are passionate about, and the things we are not so passionate about. We have to trust Him with our dreams and our realities. It is important to trust Him for what you want, it is also important to be flexible and trust that God knows what's best for us. Realize that most often we can't see His plan, which is always much greater than we could ever imagine for our lives. This is exciting, to say the least. I can imagine some pretty awesome things for my life, and to know that His plan is so much greater than my own, well, that alone gives me a reason to wake up every morning with joy.

Part of trusting God is being knowledgeable of His word. Reading His word is where His promises are revealed to you. If you speak life into a situation it will come to life. The saying, "If you can believe, you can achieve" is true because what we think about be-comes our reality. Besides, the bible says so. That is why it is important to change your mindset when negative thoughts come. If we don't know about His promises then we need to simply think about Him and ask Him to help us to change our thoughts.

A huge part of faith is trust. Therefore we need to

feed our faith by becoming knowledgeable about what He has promised in His word. As we move forward in life and continue to face challenges, faith makes them easier. We will have learned that when we walk with Him, we will still face challenges but knowing that we are never alone and that He is ultimately in control makes it easier. It may be hard for some people to believe because, when we are going through tough situations, we ask, "God, where are you?" The problems we face are sometimes very painful, but if we familiarize ourselves with His word, then we know He promises to never leave us nor forsake us! When we go through things it is either a lesson for us, or lesson for those around us; watching us go through it.

Setbacks, disappointments and even disadvantages should not cause you to feel as if you have to settle in that place. Setbacks are temporary and they are usually a set up for comebacks. It is safe to assume that when you are going through something there is a blessing on the horizon, and if that doesn't excite you I'm not sure anything will.

We know that not everyone handles stress, fear, disappointment and defeat well. However, knowing that God will give you strength in times of weakness should comfort you. So, no matter what your dilemma is, God knows you better than you know yourself. He will provide the exact amount of strength you need to overcome your obstacles!

When we focus on the wrong things it keeps us in

a place of bondage. Many people look hopelessly at their situation and feel that there is no way they can ever get out of it. If you have that attitude, then you are right about your situation. Forecasting that you are positively coming out of a situation means you are likely correct. I often tell people, you must speak life into a situation, if it's a dead thing that needs a revival then speak to it and command life. That applies to any situation you're in. Every situation, no matter how small the issue, can apply the same principles.

18.

Self-Acceptance

*"Acceptance doesn't mean resignation, it means under-
standing that something - is what it is - and there has
got to be a way through it."*
- Michael J. Fox

Self-acceptance[1] is an individual's satisfaction or
happiness with oneself. In simpler terms it means to
basically accept every aspect of one self, the good,
the bad and the ugly. We must accept our short-
comings and be aware of our weaknesses. It is all part
of getting to know ourselves and loving ourselves
despite what others say, or have said about us. When
this happens, it naturally increases our self-esteem
which allows for an increase in our happiness and
state of well-being. This is incredibly important
because many times, how we feel about ourselves is
naturally reflected in the way that we treat others.

The lack of self-acceptance is often ingrained from
childhood. If you came from a loving home, where

---

[1] American Educational Research Journal (Shepard, 1979 p.140)

your behaviors were celebrated, then it is easier for you to accept yourself. Contrast that with someone who grew up in a home where they were verbally and emotionally abused and criticized when they did not do something quite right. These behaviors not only affect children, but can positively or negatively affect their adult lives and relationships.

I've discovered that this is an important factor to discuss as it relates to obstacles. Self-acceptance is a huge obstacle for many people. One of the first steps to self-acceptance is loving yourself; no matter what. One way I choose to accept myself is, knowing that my flaws and imperfections make me an original masterpiece. So instead of allowing my scars, both internal and external, to make me feel sorry for myself, I look at the scars as an awesome alternative to what could've been. I realize how glad I am to be alive. You have to shift your focus to change the things that you really want to change. My internal, emotional scars are one component that helps shape my character. Without my experiences I would not be able to share them with others. I have learned to accept myself just as I am and realize that nothing I have gone through is by chance, but it all has a purpose. It is all being revealed to me as I pour out my heart over the pages of this book.

Self-acceptance teaches us to be balanced and allows us to practice unconditional positive regard - which is to accept a person regardless of what they have said, or done. Again this is something we must first do for ourselves. We cannot be so critical of ourselves that we cannot accept forgiveness and grow in areas which need cultivation. Sometimes we simply need to see ourselves differently and realize that we are in a constant state of growth. Often we are looking for others to give us things we don't give ourselves, such as love. People often search for love from others when they don't truly love themselves. For example, people who stay in abusive relationships for various reasons, no matter what those reasons are, it is never OK. Those who love themselves will consider that fact first, and then accept the fact that they deserve nothing less than the best. Accept yourself without reservation and know that change happens, one person at a time. Don't allow anyone make you believe that you are not awesome - you are. Let your obstacles be your stepping stones and never let them become excuses as to why you can't win.

Self-acceptance means that you are comfortable with yourself and you know who you are. You are also in touch with your strengths, your weaknesses and you own them. Part of self-acceptance is knowing your story and not being ashamed of it. After all, your story is responsible for building your character and you should never be ashamed of it. Operating in self-acceptance allows you to be free, it gives you the confidence you need to not only succeed, but to excel in life. No one can say anything negative about you or rub your failures in your face when you have already embraced them. Now, I misspoke earlier, you can't stop anyone from saying what they want about you, but you can control how you respond to it and how you allow it to make you feel. When you value yourself it is easier for others to respect who are.

Additionally, self-acceptance can improve your life. One reason is, it can eliminate issues you deal with such as: low self-esteem, victim mentality and unhappiness. It also allows you to improve yourself. When you embrace your flaws, you can confidently make strides to improve your areas of weakness. This is easier to do once you recognize that everyone has weaknesses, and we could all use improvements in multiple areas.

Self-acceptance is hard to grasp for some because of the fear that accompanies it. People don't always feel safe to reveal who they really are. They are afraid they won't be accepted by friends and family. And that is unfortunate because among family and friends is where you should find comfort. If this is not the case you should probably consider finding new friends. As aforementioned, your friends should motivate you and encourage you to be great! It is vital to surround yourself with people who will allow you to be creative and relax in who you are.

For many of us, allowing ourselves to be exposed at the most vulnerable times is a tough thing to do, but it is in those times that we can be the greatest assistance to someone who is silently suffering. When attempting to discover yourself, and gain self-acceptance, note the following issues:

1. <u>What type of relationships are you attracted to</u>?
   So many people seek out relationships they are used to. For example, if you grew up in a home where abuse was common, it may be considered normal for you. So, because it is normal for some individuals, it is not uncommon for them to seek out others who are abusers. Many people feel trapped by their past and have difficulty breaking out of their comfort zone. I wish to inspire people to try something new, dare to be different. Finally, as previously mentioned your relationships are a reflection of you, so choose your friends and associates wisely.

2. <u>How do you act when you are all alone</u>?
   When there is no one else around and you have nothing to prove to anyone, who are you? Being alone can reveal a lot about you. People who are really afraid to discover themselves never tap into that alone time. So often when we are alone, we find ourselves scrolling down someone else's timeline or twitter feed, soaking up what someone else wants us to believe about them. This is a major reason I advise people to take twenty minutes or so out of their day to focus on themselves.

   One way I self-evaluate my behavior is, when no one is looking, simply remind myself that God is watching. He sees all, so I should be on my best behavior at all times. If you feel you must behave differently, around those you should be your true self around, it causes internal chaos, otherwise known as stress, which can be harmful. It is so much easier to embrace yourself, flaws and all, so you are not overwhelmed with the responses of others when you are free to be you. If you behave in a certain manner that you've embraced and you don't plan on changing your ways, then don't be surprised by responses to the way you do things.

3. How do you look upon those who are different from you?

How do you treat people who come from a lower socio-economic background, or someone who is homeless? When I see homeless people, I usually give my last few dollars to them. There was a time when I withdrew money from the bank and sought out homeless people to hand it to. Now, I did not do this for the purpose of being able to share this with others, but I was led to do this at that time and it actually made me feel good. In contrast to that, others believe you should never give money to homeless people because they may buy drugs or alcohol with it. For those who believe that, I say, "Don't worry about what they will do with it, just follow your heart when it leads you to give to anyone."

4. <u>Stay alert to opportunities.</u>

   Are you in a constant state of readiness? When opportunity knocks do you always answer the door? If you had an option to either, do your best at a task, or take the easy way out, what choice will you make? Do you aim to soar with the eagles or will you choose to stay grounded with the chickens? Will you choose to stand out or stay with the crowd? Do you wear what everyone else does, or will you choose to have your own style? I encourage you to dare to be different. Show the world that you are one of a kind.

5. <u>The way you talk about others, when they are not around is a matter of respect.</u>

   We should always treat others how we want to be treated. Therefore we should not talk behind each other's back, and to take things one step further, you should not allow others to talk about people you care about in your presence. There should always be a question when someone tells you that "so and so was talking about you in a negative way behind your back." That question is "Why do they feel comfortable talking about me to you?" This is of extreme importance because, how you treat others, both in and out of their presence, says a lot about your character.

   These examples are not all inclusive, but to evaluate yourself by those standards is a great start to figuring out who you are. Take some time to explore yourself. I'm sure you'll be surprised by what you find. Once you complete a self-evaluation you may discover why you respond to certain things in the manner you do. As a matter of fact, you could challenge your friends to dig deeper and discover who they are as well. And if you dare, share your findings. Once you discover new things about yourself, be fully accepting of those things and embrace the new you. Hopefully, after completing this exercise you'll be released from bondage and move forward.

Networking

*"We may encounter many defeats
but we must not be defeated."*
– Maya Angelou

Networking is building relationships and making connections that are mutually beneficial for multiple parties. Networking is important to overcoming obstacles and is also why we need a diverse collection of contacts. Every person should bring value to our lives and help us meet our goals. Now I understand that networking itself can be a barrier for some people, but this is why it is important to come out of your comfort zone and start talking. You never know how a single conversation can change your life. This conversation could be with someone at work, at the library, at the mall, or a group, or an organization that you choose to volunteer with. Socializing with others you attend seminars with may be helpful, the fact that you are both attending that seminar demonstrates that you possibly have some things in common.

Networking has many beneficial components, it's not just for business. As a cancer survivor, I had the opportunity to network with other cancer patients when I was going through my treatment plan. Those relationships made things easier for me with my pink sisters. We shared remedies and practices that made it easier to cope with side effects, loneliness, emotional distress and the confusion of the medical reports. Networking is a necessary tool for living beyond your boundaries in many areas of your life. To network with someone who has been down the road you're heading is a win-win for both for all parties involved.

Meeting the right people expands your sphere of influence. Networking can be considered a full-time job. As you purposely work to get to know people, greater opportunities will occur to advance your career. I cannot express the importance of networking. You simply have to make yourself known, because if you have talents and no one knows about them, it's a lose-lose situation. We must share our gifts and talents with the world. If you are good at something, don't be afraid to brag on yourself a little. You never know, the person you were talking to could have the ability to change your life. Always be kind to each and every person you come in contact with.

Character is: qualities of honesty, courage or the like: integrity. Your trials and tribulations build your character, which is why you go through things. If you feel you are constantly going through the same type of tests, over and over again, it means you have not learned the lesson you're supposed to learn. When you respond to things in the manner pleasing to the source, you will experience elevation to another level. Acting with integrity in all situations is critical because ultimately everything we experience is a test of our faith and our character. We should look to the lesson and issues we face because it is always bigger than what we see on the surface. When we look at a body of water, we can't imagine the quantity of water because we can only see the surface, not the depth. Our obstacles have purpose and prepare us for what is to come. Many times the issues we face are building blocks that act as bridges, helping us connect from one physical place to another. Without bridges and detours we would be stuck trying to figure out the fact that when one road closes, another one opens.

God can turn around and reroute anything meant to be in your life. We must understand that before our life ever began, God completed the book of life. All the things we are going through are part of His predestined plan. We need to understand that the obstacles are part of His purpose. We are disconnecting from people in our lives and there is a reason for it. When we disconnect from our jobs, our purpose has been served there. Sometimes we need to work on a job so we can meet someone who is supposed to be in our lives. I encourage people try to and figure out why it was necessary to be in that situation at that time. Nothing in this life is supposed to last forever.

I have been taught to praise God in advance for blessings, even in trying times, praise will confuse your enemies. People on the outside looking in might expect you to be discouraged by what you are going through, but that is the farthest thing from the truth. God knows exactly what you can handle because He has equipped you to handle it by providing all the tools you need. When times get tough and situations feel like there is no way out, look to the hills for wins, it is your help.

I once heard someone say that grass doesn't *try* to grow, birds don't *try* to fly, and fish do not *try* to swim. They just do! We have to learn to just let some things happen. So often we try and force things into places where we are not meant to be. We are simply expelling a lot of energy and wasting time on things of no value. Relationships are one area that so many people struggle with, so I am going to stay here for a while.

Have you, or anyone you've ever known, poured so much of themselves into a relationship with someone who did not deserve everything they got? I'm sure the answer is yes, because it happens all the time. It all comes back to knowing your worth and deciding what you are willing and not willing to deal with. People must take a stand in relationships, because if you don't stand, you will fall.

When you were in a relationship and that person treated you in an inappropriate manner, you were partly responsible. A person can only do what you allow them to do. If you are being abused (emotionally, physically or mentally) you must make the decision to get out of that situation early. If it happens and the abuser promises to change, it's probably a lie. When asked why people stay in abusive relationships, the answer is usually love. That is a misnomer, if someone loves you, they would never hurt you and if you love yourself, you would not allow someone to hurt you. People have the meaning of love confused. The definition of love is "intense affection" (according to Webster's II dictionary).

Sadly, some people don't believe they are loved if they are not being treated inappropriately. That can sometimes be a result of their childhood and what they witnessed growing up. That is why some people struggle with relationships; they have not had a healthy example of what a relationship is supposed to be. Maybe they grew up in a household where the relationship was abusive, or they grew up in a single parent household without the opportunity to witness the roles of a husband and wife. And it became an obstacle or barrier in their adult life and romantic relationships. While I am not an expert on relation-ships, I can tell you this is an issue for those who grew up as a product of single-parent homes.

I witnessed my mom operating as the CEO of our home; she always worked independently to make things happen. This is what I witnessed growing up, this is what was normal to me, quite naturally I picked up those traits. As the CEO of my household I became independent, almost to a fault. When I entered relationships in my adult life, and the men I was involved with would share their opinion about decisions I was used to making on my own, I became easily offended. At this point I am sure that if I had come from a nuclear household, I would not have been offended and more than likely I would have appreciated their insight on the matters at hand.

While working on this project, I met someone who changed my method of thinking. From that experience I am a lot more open to the opinion of others. I am much more open to making decisions - together as one, when I am blessed enough to be married one of these days. I welcome the opportunity to bounce ideas off of others and consult with God before making decisions. It feels great, and so freeing because sometimes, like everyone else I don't have all the answers, therefore I don't always make the best decisions (we are all a work in progress). When I think of things and I don't consider all the options, it helps to be open to others opinions in order to find a balance in decision making. This never takes the place of seeking God first.

There are many reasons I look forward to one day being married, I have a young son who would benefit from the luxuries that a nuclear family provides. Stability is one, providing a positive example of what parents roles are. The opportunity to provide advice from the male and female perspective is another and the example of sharing responsibilities is so important. Some people may think that being a product of a nuclear environment is not important but the differences, versus those who are not, can be stark. This could create barriers for a couple who has been raised under different circumstances and different backgrounds - which leads me to my next point. We must have a discussion of merging two worlds or households.

Most people look at marriage as the joining of two people who love each other and come together as one, but in my eyes, it is so much more than that. It is the experiences, both good and bad, of two parties coming together as one that paints a broader picture. Consider this: a man who is 47 years old and his soon-to-be bride who is 40, together has 87 years of history merged into one night. When you look at it from that perspective it offers a different view of what marriage really is.

It is mind boggling how so many people jump into marriage without talking about their past and without really getting to know the person they vowed to spend their lives with. Hence, one of the reasons more than 55% of marriages end in divorce. Divorce is appropriate for discussion because it can be considered an obstacle. If you know the truth about these things, it may prevent you from ever going down that road; one of the goals of this project.

Some reasons people get divorced are:

1. Reasons - they get married for the wrong reasons.
2. Finances – not simply the lack of resources, but the fact that they are not financially compatible.
3. Communication – without adequate communication it is extremely difficult to resolve conflicts and a house that is divided will easily fail.
4. Lack of intimacy – this does not exactly mean sex, but we all know it's the little things that matter most - handholding, little kisses, cuddling and a hug for no reason at all.
5. Unrealistic expectations – people often believe that marriage changes people. Chances are if there was something he or she did that rubbed you the wrong way, "Yep you guessed it", marriage is not going to change that. Unmet expectations in a marriage usually lead to criticism and complaining, neither of which contributes to a healthy, satisfying relationship.
6. Lack of shared vision – some people are so blinded by love, lust and the idea of being married, that they forget to get down to the nitty-gritty of what marriage is all about.

These are not all inclusive reasons divorce happens, but they are definitely things that should be considered prior to marriage so divorce is never an obstacle you will have to face. Divorce happens much, much more than it should; after all, the traditional vows state until death do us part. I don't think that means much to anyone anymore, people stay married until they find someone else they think they like more, or until they get tired of the other person. People forget that marriage is a covenant relationship between three, God first and then individuals attempting to come together as one.

I am sure you have been in a hurry to reach a destination and while traveling you were met with an unexpected detour. It took you off course, but what could you do other than follow the detour. You couldn't be upset because there was no other option, and that's similar to life. Once obstacles come, you press through them and never say what you won't do, because life has a way of making a liar out of you. I always said I would never take chemotherapy because of the damage I have seen it cause to the body while I worked in healthcare. I felt strongly against chemo-therapy, until I was faced with cancer and that was the only option I had to prolong my life. When that barrier to health came, I didn't really have to think twice, I just prayed about it and left it in God's hands.

Many of the other things they said I would not be able to do, I have proven them wrong and continue to prove them wrong daily. I put my faith in God and not in man. I know that He and He alone is the author and finisher of my story and it doesn't have to end until He says it's done. Sometimes, when I look around, I am surprised by all the cancer-causing agents out there, but one can take all the precautions and remedies in the world and still succumb to illness, pain and suffering. Instead of trying to spend so much time trying to beat the clock, I encourage you to simply enjoy each day and treat it as a gift. Every time we open our eyes to a new day we should feel like we are unwrapping a gift; it truly is. So often we take life for granted.

We need to live life without limits, beyond boundaries. More often than not, we are so careful in our approach to things, we play it safe. Playing it safe will never get us to a place of ecstasy because it will never allow us to step outside of the box. People who play it safe would not be entrepreneurs who invent new things for people to enjoy or products to use or services that make life easier. When I spoke of living without limits, it is a challenge that allows you to release the shackles that have held you bound. Life beyond boundaries allows you to step into new dimensions and live outside of the box.

Living in the box and living with limits are obstacles within themselves, so, in order for you to overcome them, you can begin to socialize with people who are different from you. You'd be surprised by the things you can learn from them. We all come from diverse backgrounds and the values that have been instilled in us from an early age shape our values and have a huge influence on the decisions and choices we make.

Failure

*"No human ever became interesting by not failing.
The more you fail and recover and improve, the better
you are as a person. Ever meet someone who's always
had everything work out for them with zero struggle?
They usually have the depth of a puddle.
Or they don't exist."
- Chris Hardwick*

Failure is an important part of life and is necessary for success. Actually, it's one of life's most important teachers. It is through failure while dealing with some of our life issues, that our personality is shaped. Sometimes failure hurts. The pain is to drive you towards your goal. Your journey will be filled with trials, tribulations, upsets, setbacks and failures. Failure is ok as long as we learned a lesson from it, you get up, dust yourself off and try again. With failure comes growth. Our experiences allow us to improve. Painful situations are usually the most memorable. When failure comes, naturally the first thing that people want to do is to give up and while that might be the easiest thing to do, giving up is never a wise option. You should always remember that if you fail at something once or twice, continue on until you succeed. Ultimately you should fail your way to success - it is possible.

Failure can help you discover yourself. Remember, I applied for more than 200 jobs after receiving my Bachelor's degree. I didn't realize that all that rejection was designed to push me into my true destiny. It was never about those jobs, it was all about making a name for myself and being my own boss. I was not designed to work for an employer; however, I was designed to work for you, the person reading this book. I was designed to inspire you. Keeping you inspired gives my life great purpose. Even though I have always been in a position to motivate, mentor and inspire people, I am disappointed that it took a horrific tragedy of illness, before I decided to fully immerse myself in purpose. Although I was disappointed, I am still grateful that it is not too late to get it done. I know that God makes no mistakes, so the timing is significant, because His timing is perfect. I discovered my purpose exactly when I was supposed to. Motivation is my passion and it feels good to serve.

Additionally, failure can be looked on as a steppingstone to success, if you focus on learning a lesson versus sulking in the fact that you failed a task. Most people who are successful have an arsenal of cfailures and can share with others what led to their eventual success. Failure can be a barrier or obstacle depending on how you look at it, but the way to overcome the issue is to look at it objectively. In order to do that, you must analyze it and accept it as such. Many individuals think success comes easy, every failure is a building block to success. It is not enough to just become successful, you have to continue working hard to stay there.

Even in the face of adversity and failure you should never give up. As aforementioned, you should always consider the fact that perseverance pays off. We should all understand that on the way to success and accomplishing our goals, there will be challenges, mistakes and errors. The key component is to keep pushing in spite of what things look like. There are a few examples of famous figures I would like to share with you. These individuals failed on countless occasions before reaching their desired outcome.

1. Henry Ford -- famously known for inventing the assembly line and American made cars: Before accomplishing this arduous task he'd attempt-ted several other business ventures before founding Ford Motor Company.
2. Colonel Sanders of Kentucky Fried Chicken, now known as KFC – his famous chicken recipe was rejected more than 1000 times before being accepted by a restaurant.
3. Thomas Edison – a successful inventor made 1000 unsuccessful attempts at creating the

lightbulb, before he discovered a design that worked. Where would we be in relation to light, if he had given up?

4. Oprah Winfrey – had a rough childhood and several occupational setbacks, one that included being fired from a television anchor position because she was unfit for T.V. Now she owns her OWN television network and is on television almost daily in some form.

5. Theodor Suess Giesel – the author of many well-known Dr. Suess books, had his first book rejected by 27 publishers.

6. Steven King – his first book received 30 rejections from publishers which caused him to throw the manuscript in the trash, luckily his wife pulled it from the trash and encouraged him to resubmit it. He is now known as one of the best-selling authors, of all times with hundreds of books and several movies.

7. Michael Jordon – arguably one of the best basketball players of all time stated the following, "I've missed more than 9000 shots in my career. I have lost almost 300 games. On 26 occasions I have been entrusted to take the game winning shot and I missed. I have failed over and over again in my life, and that is why I succeed."

So you see I have provided a few examples of people who rejected failure and chose to win. Now, what is your excuse......I'll wait....

If they can do the things mentioned above, then you can certainly accomplish your goals. These people are no different from us, they had gifts and talents on the inside of them and they chose to tap into their potential. It is my pleasure to inform you that you have greatness inside of you, that you are special, that you can do it. Pursue your passion, you can really be your own boss, and you could be a millionaire! How does that sound? Did you already know these things about yourself? If not, please believe all of the things I have just spoken over your life because they are indeed true.

21.

Times Up!

"Change your thoughts and you change your world."
- Norman Vincent Peale

During the time I was writing this book, which is dedicated to my mom, I lost her. She passed on before I had the opportunity to finish it. It would have been nice for her to have had the opportunity to add my book to the collection of books she had on her shelf. I know she would have been proud to see the completed book. Now, she will watch from heaven and although I miss her deeply, I am thankful she is not suffering in pain anymore. My loss is certainly bittersweet, but people often misunderstand that it is not about quantity of life, but more importantly, it is about the quality of life. What my mom was doing the last year of her life wasn't living. She was miserable and that made me sadder than actually losing her when she passed away. It was more like freedom; with dementia and limited activity she became a prisoner in her own body. After dementia was diagnosed she wasn't the person I knew her to be all these years. Over the last year we became distant, which was extremely difficult for me, I felt like I lost my best friend. She was someone that I could share my deepest darkest secrets with. Those relationships are hard to come by. I could tell her anything and she never looked at me differently.

Dealing with loss is difficult and is normally a stressful time. It is a time of uncertainty for loved ones left behind. Many times, when it comes to death, loved ones are selfish and may have selfish reasons for wanting their loved one to stay alive. When you really love someone, you must love them enough to let them go when it is time. This is what happened to my mom, she was ill and had been suffering for a long period of time, so when she became critically ill it was easy for me to make the decision to limit her care when it was time. Now, my brother on the other hand, had difficulty with the decision.

For him, it was because she became his sugar momma and his reasons for keeping her alive had everything to do with her ability to financially support him. So when it came time to make the decision to limit her care, he wanted the doctors to do everything possible to keep her alive. I was devastated that he could actually consider keeping her alive in the state she was in and the poor prognosis that existed. I expressed my disgust to the nurse and she shared a story with me about another patient whose family kept her alive until her fingers began to fall off in the bed from gangrene and poor circulation. It was so bad; the ethics committee had to get involved.

According to the nurse, it was apparent the family did not have her best interest at heart. Who would allow their loved one to live under those conditions? Although she wasn't supposed to share the experience of that other family with me, she was just assuring me that I wasn't alone and this was not an uncommon occurrence within families. After our discussion I could not help but think, "How unfair to that poor soul and others who have to go through this same experience".

22.

Now that We're Here…

My theme of late has been, cancer changed my life so I would have the opportunity to change the lives of others. Many people have such a narrow view of what life is supposed to be, that they never really live. Once you reach your milestone goals, enjoy the moment! Celebrate the fact that you have turned the vision into a reality. This is worth celebrating since so many do not accomplish their goals. The celebration is especially necessary if you've completed a goal you doubted would come to fruition. Then, you want to share it with the world, not to rub it in their faces, but to demonstrate that dreams really do come true! Another reason you want to share it is because you want to prove all the naysayers wrong – those who doubted your abilities. I share this with students when someone says you can't do something, instead of debating with them, show them that you can. Actions speak louder than words. After reaching some of your dreams and goals and you confidently prepare to set another goal, here are some things to consider:

- What methods did you use to make the last dream a reality?
- What did your last experience teach you?
- Are you prepared for setbacks?
- How do you overcome challenges?
- Who was your support team?
- How can you help someone else?

Another vital point to remember is, while continuing on the journey in pursuit of your dreams - remain focused. And never forget about other priorities in your life. While reaching for your goals, you do not want other areas of your life to suffer; namely your spouse, children, family and friends. You must remember those important relationships because you want them to still be viable when you meet your goals. It is easy for people to feel forgotten or feel like they have been sacrificed, as a result of you attempting to reach your goals.

As previously mentioned, it is important to enjoy every step of the journey. Many people are miserable as they go through life, seeking to reach their end goal. As a matter of fact, we are often so focused on our goals we miss the important things in life, things that should bring us immeasurable memories. The way you live your life en-route to your destiny requires your intense attention to detail. So often I say, during motivational talks with students, you have to be grateful for all of your experiences since they all have purpose. Too often we wait for things to be perfect before we rejoice and be glad. In actuality, we need to be grateful and celebrate the small things in life. It is a blessing each time we wake up and we should be thankful for the use of our limbs, the ability to think straight, to make our own decisions, etc. That old saying, "You don't miss something until you lose it" is so true. Please take this as a reminder to enjoy the small things. Although it is important to stay focused on your dreams, it is of equal importance to welcome the journey and celebrate each obstacle you overcome along the way.

Troubles will come, there is no doubt about that but when challenges come, and you know they are coming, here are some things you can do to modify the way you think about them:

- Take action - do something related to your troubles that push the limits.
- Seek out challenges - simply because you now know they build character.
- Construct a team - seek out people who will help you reach your goals by monitoring your progress and keeping you accountable.
- Remain focused - keep your mind set on positive things, when negativity comes, counter punch it.

- Think on purpose - allow everything you need to come to you. Take at least 20 minutes a day to visualize those things that you need in order to be successful.
- Be still - you'll be amazed at the number of things that happen and the infinite number of ideas that will arise.
- Err on the side of confidence - always walk upright, hold your head high and maintain that look of confidence, even when there is doubt.
- Celebrate your wins - when situations look dire and you don't know how you are going to make it, make a list of all the issues you've made it through in the past.

Sometimes obstacles exist and we don't even realize they are there. Often some of the largest obstacles exist in our minds and if we could simply change our mindsets and the way we think about things, we could be so much further along than we are. Many times we miss the mark because we are so distracted by life. For example, you may be so busy at work you don't realize, that job is not your passion, and it is actually blocking you from accomplishing your purposeful goal. Let's say that you have a goal of starting your own business but because you are giving so much time and attention to a cause that helps someone else accomplish their goals, time and life passes you by. Before you know it, years have gone by and you haven't acted on those things in your heart. This is why occasionally, at least every six months or so, you should re-evaluate your goals. If you are not on task, now is the time you need to refocus and come into alignment with what you need to do. If you are on task, push yourself to be greater, never remain satisfied.

23.

Final Note

"Love the moment and the energy of that moment
will spread beyond boundaries."
- Corita Kent

To everything there is a season. There is a time to mourn, there is a time to cry, there is a time for sadness, there is a time for happiness, there is a time for love. Know when your season starts and ends. Have an open mind, knowing that seasons change and believe that God gives you grace to travel through each season. While going through never forget the lessons along the way. One of the most important things to remember when facing challenges is that if you are still breathing, you still have a reason to press on. Trust God, He is the truth to living beyond boundaries.

24.

Food for Thought

I've included quotes from various people who have motivated me at one time or another. Hopefully, you will read through and find those that inspire you in difficult times or while overcoming obstacles.

- "The best preparation for tomorrow is doing your best today." - H. Jackson Brown, Jr
- "The darkest hour, only has 60 minutes" – Morris Mandale
- "You miss 100 percent of the shots you never take." - Wayne Gretzky
- "People often say that motivation doesn't last. Well, neither does bathing – that's why we recommend it daily." - Zig Ziglar
- "Put your heart, mind and soul into even your smallest acts. This is the secret to success." – Swami Sivananda
- "I can't change the direction of the wind, but I can adjust my sails to always reach my destination" – Jimmy Dean
- "You are what you believe yourself to be." - Paulo Coelho
- "Nothing is impossible, the word itself says "I'm possible." – Audrey Hepburn

- "Someone is sitting in the shade today because someone planted a tree a long time ago."
  – Warren Buffet
- Just do it. – Nike
- "If opportunity doesn't knock, build a door."
  - Milton Berle
- "The power of imagination makes us infinite."
  - John Muir
- "The things that we love tell us what we are."
  - Thomas Aquinas
- "Your big opportunity may be right where you are now." - Napoleon Hill
- "Follow your bliss and the universe will open doors where there were only walls." – Joseph Campbell
- From a small seed a mighty trunk may grow."
  –Aeschylus
- "Give light, and the darkness will disappear of itself." - Desiderius Eramus
- "Out of difficulties grow miracles." - Jean de la Bruyere
- "The measure of who we are is what we do with what we have." - Vince Lombardi
- "The best way out is always through." - Robert Frost
- "Don't raise your voice, improve your argument." – Desmond Tutu
- "Prayer is man's greatest power! - W. Clement Stone
- "Winners focus on winning. Losers focus on Winners." – Eric Thomas
- "A champion is someone who gets up when he can't. – Jack Dempsey

- "Attitude is a little thing that makes a big difference." - Winston Churchill
- "Be faithful in small things because it is in them that your strength lies." - Mother Teresa
- "Excellence is not a skill, it's an attitude." - Ralph Marston
- "The only disability in life is a bad attitude." --Scott Hamilton
- "Courage is knowing what not to fear." – Plato
- "It takes courage to grow up and become who you are." – E.E. Cummings
- "When you have a dream, you've got to grab it and never let it go." - Carol Burnett
- "Winners are not afraid of losing. But losers are. Failure is part of the process of success. People who avoid failure also avoid success." - Robert T. Kiyosaki
- "You build on failure. You use it as a stepping stone. Close the door on the past. You don't try to forget the mistakes, but you don't dwell on it. You don't let it have any of your energy, or any of your time, or any of your space." - Johnny Cash
- "It's not how far you fall, but how high you bounce that counts." - Zig Ziglar
- "Failure is so important. We speak about success all the time. It is the ability to resist failure or use failure that often leads to greater success. I've met people who don't want to try for fear of failing." - J.K. Rowling
- "When you focus on being a blessing, God makes sure that you are always blessing in abundance." – Joel Osteen

- "Don't let someone who gave up on their dreams talk you out of yours." – Zig Ziglar
- "Want to succeed as bad as you want to breathe." - Eric Thomas
- "Setting goals is the first step in turning the invisible into the visible." --Tony Robbins
- "Set your goals high, and don't stop till you get there." – Bo Jackson
- "The way to get started is to quit talking and begin doing." – Walt Disney
- "Either you run the day or the day runs you." –Jim Rohn
- "Survival was my only hope, success my only revenge." - Patricia Cornwell
- "Failure isn't fatal, but failure to change might be." - John Wooden
- "Everything you want is on the other side of fear." - Jack Canfield
- "Success is most often achieved by those who don't know that failure is inevitable." - Coco Chanel
- "Only those who dare to fail greatly can ever achieve greatly." - Robert F. Kennedy
- "The phoenix must burn to emerge." - Janet Fitch
- "To the mind that is still, the whole universe surrenders. – Lao Tzu
- "One of the greatest values of mentors is the ability to see ahead what others cannot see and help them to navigate a course to their destination." – John C. Maxwell
- "When we give ourselves permission to fail, we, at the same time, give ourselves permission to excel." - Eloise Ristad

- Our chief want in life is someone who will make us do what we can." – Ralph Waldo Emerson

Pure Motivation

The following positive statements represent what life has to offer you. As you read through them, be motivated by them and repeat them, until you believe them!

- Refuse to be defeated.
- Yes you can.
- Realize your full potential.
- Have unshakable confidence.
- Chase your dreams until you win.
- Focus on what matters.
- Don't worry, God is always on time.
- Don't let anything stop you.
- Live in the world you dream of.
- Make every second count.
- Think big.
- Dream big.
- You are your biggest enemy.
- Write a book.
- Don't be scared to make a mistake.
- You can have what you want.
- Never stop growing.
- Pursue your goal.

- Make goals that will take you out of your comfort zone.
- Make it happen.
- Opportunity is waiting for you.
- Find a reason to move forward.
- What drives you?
- You are great.
- Stay strong.
- Allow your pain to push you.
- Push yourself.
- Say yes to your future.
- Excellence is a habit.
- Be the best that you can be.
- Protect your dreams.
- If you want something go get it.
- Finish the race.
- Keep moving forward.
- Know your worth.
- Show the world how great you are.
- Develop a positive vision.
- Believe in yourself.
- You have a choice.
- Today is a new beginning.
- Take chances.
- Make mistakes it's OK.
- Failure is part of success.
- Positive thinking can achieve the impossible.
- Ask for help if you need it.
- Try new things and challenges.
- Be patient.
- Don't be afraid to start over.
- Nothing worth having comes easy.
- Create opportunities.

- Never be satisfied with yourself.
- You're responsible for your success.
- Build your own business.
- Never lose hope.
- Live your dreams.
- Don't let social media control you.
- You have a great future ahead of you.
- Be better than you were yesterday.
- Believe the best is yet to come.
- Don't be lazy.
- Don't give up.
- Your dream is a reality.
- Focus on winning.
- Money does not define you.
- Never settle.
- Build your legacy.
- Look for opportunities.
- Take risk.
- You will not lose.
- Make your own rules.
- Don't be afraid to fail.
- Value your time.
- You will never fail.
- When you fall simply get back up.
- Live your dreams.
- Be a leader.
- You can succeed.
- Transform your life.
- Hold your head high.
- There is no substitute for hard work.
- Look within, you'll find success.
- Don't let your friends tell you what to do.
- Start now.

- Don't wait for things to be perfect.
- You are better than average.
- Fear nothing.
- Be free.
- Don't waste your activities.
- Act now.
- Never throw in the towel.
- Act on your ideas.
- Develop yourself.
- Be with people who want more.
- You will experience setbacks but keep going.
- You are greater than your circumstances.

26.

I AM

So often we have a tendency to listen to what songs, social media, our peers and other people have to say about us. Listed below are words that I believe describe you. Repeat after me:

"I AM _____"

Fearless	Successful
Unstoppable	Awesome
Brilliant	Original
Empowered	Authentic
Royalty	Prosperous
Special	Magnificent
Fantastic	Masterpiece
Pro-active	Custom made
Intelligent	Champion
Creative	Dependable
Perfect	Peaceful
Insightful	Free
Unlimited	Overcomer
Radiant	Inspired

Valuable	Worthy
Important	Blessed
Dynamic	Enough
Unique	Great
Genuine	Capable
Strong	Courageous
Gifted	NOT AN ACCIDENT

27.

Excerpts from Student Letters

I have had the privilege of speaking to thousands of youth in various locations through my experience as a substitute teacher, at various events and other forums. Usually, I ask the students to either write a quick letter or send an email if they have been inspired by anything I have said. I have included a limited number of responses that I received. These responses liter-ally keep me going and allow me to recognize that my labor is not in vain. To all of you who have shared your feedback, I say thank you. It just goes to show you, if you give positive – you get positive.

"Thank you for being so inspiring. I will never forget you!"

"You inspire me to do better and forget what my past did to me."

"I think that you are really inspiring and I'm sure that it has changed a lot of people. And that it will change a lot more too. I love how you told us all the things that you have studied in college, although you are not doing any of them BUT what you're passionate about."

"You're making a difference and saving lives."

"You had a very inspiring story. If you told that story to jail prisoners they would turn their lives around."

"To the best person I know: I want you to know that you are a hero to many. You never give up, you always keep going. And you have taught me to do the same. Don't give up. You taught everyone the importance of living to the fullest."

"You showed me today that there is no such thing as outgrowing your ambition."

"Listening to you speak was a great motivational experience."

"I think you changed my life around."

"I just wanted to say that you are really strong and I'm proud of you for trying to change people's lives."

"I want to thank you for letting me realize how important I am in this crazy world. I am 1 of a kind and unique. I think that it is time for me to write a new chapter in my life. Thank you!"

"Thanks for your words, I have thought about my decisions. I know now I need to think more about myself....So thank you so much."

"Thank you for sharing your story, thank you for motivating people and making them feel better about themselves."

"Thank you for telling people it gets better."

"I really loved what you said today, I have been feeling down and today I'm not the best and that speech really helped."

"Your words were just what I needed right now."

"Thank you for telling me that I can get through (hard times) it means a lot to me. Thank you so much and I wish you the best of luck."

"Words cannot explain what you have done for me today. I don't show emotional much at all. I was close to crying today."

"You really touched my heart."

"I woke up with stormy clouds in my head and your story cleared my head and brought light to it. I thank you so much for it."

"You are my role model, you showed me that I can do whatever I want because nothing is impossible."

"Your words and your story have not only touched my heart but gave me the courage to stand and fight for my life... You have inspired me to live my life with pride."

"I loved hearing your opinion; your words can motivate people all around the world."

"Ms. Stringer, you are amazing."

"These words will change me forever."

"You are an amazing person who inspires so many young people."

"I wish I could put you in my pocket and take you everywhere I go."

"Thank you so much for this speech it helped me tremendously."

"Keep doing what you are doing, you are amazing."

"Thanks for making my day better and changing my outlook on life.

"I want to encourage you to keep up your ministry."

"Keep Inspiring."

"I hope your words reach as many people as possible and they motivate everyone to be the best they can be."

"Thank you for the greatest hour ever."

About the Author…

Malissa Stringer is an author who has had to overcome many obstacles in her life. She was born to a single mother and did not discover who her father was until she was 19 years old. She actually met him when she was 38 years old. She was raised by her Godmother who was not only a mother to her but doubled as a best friend. Malissa lost her mother during the writing of her first project *Living Beyond Boundaries by Overcoming Obstacles.*

Malissa often visited the home of her biological mother, where she was first sexually molested at the age of three. This event caused her to be emotionally scarred for years. Malissa was the only child of five who was given up to be raised outside of her mother's home.

At age 12, she tragically lost a brother who was beaten to death. At age 19, she nearly drowned after falling out of a canoe during a company picnic, but that was not the end. Malissa continue working for a few more years before taking the plunge into college. She started working on a degree in Criminal Justice because of her heart to help others. After completing that, she went on to complete her Bachelors in Business Management and finally completed her Masters in Legal Studies, two days after her 36th birthday.

A year later she was diagnosed with breast cancer at the facility she worked for. Unfortunately, the diagnosis was delayed 22 months which required her to undergo the most extreme treatment. Malissa fought the battle with cancer and she won!

Talk about overcoming obstacles and beating the odds, her story continues on. Stay tuned for details! Her story is like a fine wine, it gets better with time. She has had mountains to climb, but when the going gets tough - she gets tougher.

You can reach Malissa via:

Email: MCSpeaks1@gmail.com

🐦 :   MCSpeaks1

Website: www.MalissaStringer.com

Instagram: MCSpeaks 1

If this book has inspired you in any way, please consider purchasing it as a gift for someone you care about.

Thank you for reading this book; I hope it was as much a pleasure to read, as it was to write!

CPSIA information can be obtained
at www.ICGtesting.com
Printed in the USA
FFOW02n0053100717
37511FF